THANKS SCF

Heart And Soul

Heart And Soul

Carol Decker

As told to Andy Richardson

First published in Great Britain in 2016 by A Way With Media Ltd, Shrewsbury, SY3 7LN

Copyright © Carol Decker 2016

The author and publisher are grateful to the *Shropshire Star* for permission to reproduce photographs.

A CIP catalogue record for this book is available from the British Library.

ISBN 9781910469002

Editor, publisher: Andy Richardson
Editorial production: David Briggs
Editorial proofing: Rachel Jones

Printed and bound by 1010 Printing Group Ltd, China.

www.awaywithmedia.com

For Richard, Scarlett and Dylan

Chapters

Home From Home

I was born in Huyton in the middle of Liverpool. I still have extended family there. I am spiritually a Scouser at heart, I suppose. Once a Scouser, always a Scouser: they claim you. We lived in a grey, squat council block and each night we would hear the neighbours fighting through the wall. The block was next to a bit of tatty old land with a donkey on it. I've never forgotten that donkey.

Huge tracts of Liverpool had been bombed and across town and in Stoneycroft, where my Nana Healey lived, whole corners had gone. I was born in 1957, little more than 10 years after the war. Liverpool still struggles to this day to be regenerated, so it was pretty shocking back then; it was seared in my mind as a place that was over – flattened. People were poor. People were struggling. The shipping industry was on the decline. That once proud city seemed to be dying. I remember thinking even at a very young age that I wanted to live somewhere that was beginning.

We were from a working class background. My Mum was one of seven, Irish Catholic, and my Dad was one of two, English Protestant with some long-time-ago Dutch blood, hence the surname. He had a sister called Beryl. My Nana Decker was a tall woman with jet-black hair and dark brown eyes, just like my Dad. She was the manageress of a fruit and veg shop; back then in the 1950s that was no mean feat. She was quite a trailblazer. I used to want to impress her and gain her approval. She was a bit of a Tartar, a very tough woman who frightened the crap out of my Mum when my parents were first married. In 1956 my Mum and Dad had to be married in a side altar in the Catholic Church. There were no flowers and no choir. Purple cloths were draped over the statues. My Mum was marrying in shame, Dad was not a Catholic!

The mutual enmity existed on both sides of the family. As far as my hoity-toity Grandma Decker was concerned, my Dad was marrying a lower class left-footer. Mum's family considered my Nana Decker a snob and my Nana Decker considered them as beneath her. There was no love lost between them and never any big happy family get-togethers with the two sides mixing. As well as being disaffected with one another, the two families were across a great religious divide. Their relationships soured my view of religion. Early on in my life my overall impression of the church/religion was that it divided people. It created prejudice that parents passed down to their kids. I didn't want any part of it so I opted out early when I was 10. We had by then moved to Wellington, in Shropshire. Mum had continued to send me and my brother to church. Aged 10, I confessed, well I was Catholic, to my Mum that not only did I not want to go to church anymore but that I had been spending my collection plate money in the sweet shop. Oh God I was going to burn. Mum just looked at me for what seemed like an eternity and then said 'Okay but don't tell Nana.'

Until her death in the mid '70s the family spent a lot of time concealing things from Nana Healey. And I swear if the poor woman had put all the money she spent on lighting candles in the church into a savings account she could've lived in a mansion and not a council house. Devout as she was, almost every sentence started with 'Jesus, Mary and Joseph'. We lived in a flat over a parade of shops opposite Yates's Wine Lodge. When I was two-and-a-half-years-old and Mum was pregnant with my brother Gary we were evicted, chucked out onto the street because we couldn't afford the rent. They didn't care what happened to you; there were no rights for tenants or anything like that. We were evicted on the spot and our stuff went on the pavement while Dad was at work. Apart from the sheer upset of that happening while Mum was alone it was utterly humiliating in front of the neighbours. She had to go to Nana Decker's, cap in hand.

Nana Decker allowed us to live with her in her house in Liverpool Road. She absolutely terrified my Mum and used her as a bit of a skivvy. She would be very critical of any household chore she did. My Mum had a really tough time in the early days of her marriage. With no money of her own and two little kids she had to take the situation she was in. She had no choice.

I remember my Nana being an intimidating woman who could be very condescending. If on a roll of pontification, no interruptions were brooked. Her eyes would roll into the top of her head and her eyelids would sort of spasm. Then there was the Decker Finger. That would involve her right middle finger being firmly poked into the nearest available surface, to emphasize a point, resulting in a loud tapping noise. The Decker Finger and eye rolling was genetically passed onto my Dad and his sister Beryl. The three of them together resembled a small group of twitching crazy people trying to communicate with the spirit world.

Nana Decker had a front parlour that was out of bounds to us children. I don't think it was ever used. If I did sneak in I didn't stay for long for fear of breathing on something that might break. The room had a nice collection of art deco ornaments in fancy glass cabinets, a stark contrast to my impoverished Nana Healey's house, which also had a front room for Sunday best or a visiting priest.

Nana Decker had an old biscuit tin full of broken paste jewellery for me to play with. I am still a magpie to this day, attracted to sparkly stuff. I keep my own jewellery in haphazard heaps. I like to rummage through it like treasure. I like my stuff to surprise me. 'Oh my God I forgot I had that!' That comes from the days of Nana's tin.

She also had a miniature poodle called Peppy who bit everybody. The little fucker would sneak behind the settee and sink its teeth into your hand if you let it dangle down the side. Peppy was never sufficiently chastised for biting her grandchildren, oh no, it was our fault for letting our hands dangle down when we knew what could happen. Eventually Peppy went mad and attacked Nana, biting her viciously on the leg when she was alone. She had to club it to death with a carriage clock off the mantelpiece. Good riddance I thought, wish I could've joined in the beating.

Years later my father stopped speaking entirely to his mother and sister Beryl, not even reconciling before her death. I think I have that side of the family running through my veins as I too can be very unforgiving when crossed. I am part cheery, sociable Scouser; part vengeful Mafioso.

My Grandpa Decker was a sailor in the merchant navy and had died of cancer three months before I was born. Obviously I never met him, but my Dad would start many a sentence with 'you would have loved your Granddad'. He was away at sea a lot. I don't think my Dad could've seen that much of him, but when he returned I think he spoiled them and therefore my Dad had an heroic memory of him. He drank like a fish, as I understand it. I inherited that gene too!

Granddad Healey also liked a drink. My memories of him are of a small, gentle man, softly spoken, who only left his armchair to go to the pub, which of course drove Nana Healey mad. I once wrote to him inviting him to Shropshire, when we had moved. I got a lovely letter politely declining, with drawings of a bowl for my goldfish and a saucer of food for my cat, Peaches. I still have it in a box. Granddad had worked on the docks. It was a hard job unloading all the ships but Mum said in those austere times they often had an exotic fruit like a banana to eat that had 'accidentally' fallen in to his pocket. I know from family stories that due to the drink he had not always been the most attentive of fathers or the most devoted husband but he was nothing but sweet to me.

When he died we all went back to Liverpool. There were dozens of us. We have a large extended family who enjoy a special get together. A funeral means a knees up and free food and drink - after an appropriate amount of crying, of course!

It was a good turnout. The priest had a new public address system and microphone that loudly amplified his voice around an already cavernous, vaulted, echoing church. This resulted in his first sentence still travelling around the church as he began the next one. It became a canon of indistinguishable accolades to my Granddad, reducing me and my cousins to hysterical tears of shoulder-shaking, silent laughter. His voice is possibly still bouncing off the walls today.

The furniture in Nana Decker's house was very big and dark. There were big dark brown wardrobes and loud clocks ticking in the heavy silence with no comforting background noise of a radio or TV. There were militarily straight candlewick bedspreads and big thick eiderdowns made of shiny cold material on the beds. You had to go past Granddad's room to reach the toilet. It was still kept as if he was due home and I thought that his ghost was in there. I'd never met him and I was terrified to go up there. A lot of that was down to my Catholicism because of my other Nana. Nana Healy, was a total fire-and-brimstone Catholic. I was terrified of the dead and God. I was dragged along to Holy Communion and mass all in Latin. Naturally we were all fluent in Latin in working class Liverpool. Such was the pompous attitude of the church back then that it didn't matter that we, the great unwashed in the pews, didn't understand a sodding word. I don't go to church anymore and I don't believe in God, I never did even as a child – not in any God that's ever been explained to me. Nana Healey had a Bible with this illustration of Purgatory, the Catholic holding tank. It was similar to Michelangelo's creation of man where the hands nearly touch. There was a naked man with flames up to his waist, reaching up in terror and pain with the most agonized expression on his face and an angel above him stretching down trying to do his best to get him out of there. And my Nana Healey would say: 'And you'll go there if you don't eat your peas!' Talk about swatting a fly with a sledgehammer.

Fire and brimstone zealous Catholicism, gives you a very dramatic childhood. There's lots of imagery – crucifixes, beads, angels, the devil, flames, cloying smells of frankincense and myrrh, Purgatory, Limbo and of course Hell: it's all very Dante. I was already very afraid of the dark and the dead and what might happen to my worthless soul. I didn't really know where my Grandpa Decker was. Was he burning somewhere? Was he in that room? Where do dead Protestants go? I was very scared of the whole thing.

I was also spooked out when the streetlight shone through the bedroom window of our flat in Huyton. At a certain angle the light made a face on the curtains. I used to call for my Mum to look at it and she used to show me that it was just shadows. When I was younger, I had a lot of dreams where I would astral-plane. It stopped as I got older, which was a shame. Your subconscious stops being so creative. The top third of the door of my Nana Decker's house was stained glass and the sun would shine through in all different colours and hit the parquet floor in the hall. I would astral-plane down her stairs in my dreams even though I did not live there nor had we ever stayed the night. In my dreams, I would see all the colours, extra vivid, hitting the ground. Those are two of the strongest memories associated with my childhood in Liverpool: a fear of the dead and flying in my dreams. Finally we did get relocated into a council block and our own flat, which was next to a donkey on some scrap land in Huyton. It was obviously better than having to live with your Tartar-of-a-mother-in-law. But you could hear the neighbours arguing and some of the kids were rough to say the least. There was one kid called Chris who persuaded me to pick up a sleepy wasp; yes, okay I was a tad gullible. Naturally it stung me so I picked up a log and belted Chris around the head, concussing him. There was also an attempt to squash a small girl into a suitcase to see if she'd fit. I was sort of involved in that too, which is horrific! It makes me shudder in shame. But kids sometimes end up going along with the pack. We were a bit like the children in Lord Of The Flies.

Life was hard for my Dad. He took three jobs and went to night-school to study business. His intention was to get us out of Liverpool. It was time to get the hell out of Dodge before I ended up on the road to GBH. He had jam butties in his lunch box, which he used to eat away from the other workers so they couldn't see that he didn't have any meat or anything substantial in his sandwiches. When he did have meat my Dad used to have tongue and brawn sandwiches, pig's trotters and sweetbreads. We were poor; we couldn't afford to have proper meat; we had to have the bits that they shit out of and ate with in your sandwiches.

But now you go to a fancy restaurant in London and offal will be served with some amazing jus. You often find that the food of the poor becomes some trendy cuisine. I still won't eat anything's balls, brains or tongue though.

Dad would also have little entrepreneurial episodes, like the time he covered every available surface in our flat with trays of toffee apples to sell on the truck. He made the toffee himself, dunked about 200 apples and put them all to set on the trays before we went to bed. The next morning all the toffee had run off the apples and set flat on the trays with the apples stuck down in it. Poor Dad, he had to dump all those precious apples, but my brother and I had more toffee than you can shake a stick at.

Although not well off, I don't remember going without anything. At Christmas my parents would creep in and put presents at the end of the bed. My Dad had a Santa suit and we were told that you got a cabbage or cauliflower left at the end of the bed as a penalty if you spied on Santa. One night I couldn't sleep for excitement and my Dad had come in from the pub, a bit tiddly. He put on the Santa suit, and placed socks with tangerines and nuts in at the foot of our beds.

Through my lashes I saw a shadow moving across the room. I was terrified that Santa would know that I'd spied and I would get a cabbage. My brother and I woke up at something like 5.30am on Christmas morning, as you do when you're young and excited. There was nothing at the end of our beds but fruit and nuts in a sock. I thought there were no presents because I'd spied on Santa. So we went running into our parents' room screaming our heads off. Of course what they'd done was bought us gifts that year that were too big to lug into the room; they'd left them all in the lounge. I'd got a big cot and a dolly while my brother – and they regretted this in about 20 minutes – got a drum kit.

Going out as a family was a different thing then. Kids weren't allowed in pubs and the pub was a big part of life in Liverpool. I remember often sitting in the car with my brother and my Mum. Dad would come out with crisps and lemonade but my poor old Mum had to sit in the car with us. There was no going in as a family. There was always a saloon bar and the off licence. The saloon bars had frosted-out windows like there was something going on in there that you weren't supposed to see. The lounge was where you sat with your girlfriend until you married her. After the wedding you'd go back into the saloon bar with your mates and she'd have to go and sit outside in the car with the kids.

Dad worked really hard and finally got a job in a small supermarket called Waterworths, in Wellington, in Shropshire. That gave us our chance to get out of the council block in Liverpool. I was seven. Wellington couldn't have been more different. It was a small rural market town and we moved to a new-build housing estate. Our house, 53 Hordley Road, was a three bed semi-detached with a front and back garden; it cost around £2,500 and Dad had to have a mortgage. Oh my God I spend that on shoes! We were going up in the world. I settled awkwardly into the local school, St Patrick's Catholic Infant and Juniors. I had a broad Liverpudlian accent and I was very skinny with orange hair, round National Health glasses and a patch over a lazy left eye. I also had buckteeth. The teacher introduced me to a very unenthusiastic class. There wasn't a queue to get to know or sit by the new girl.

My little brother Gary fared better. He was good at sports and made friends easily. He was a very beautiful little boy. He had twinkling hazel eyes, a smattering of Anne Of Green Gables' freckles across his nose, white-blond hair and butter wouldn't melt in that perfect mouth of his. My Mum adored him – what is it about Mums and their sons? – and if he had done something wrong he would lie through his teeth or blame me in front of her. She would always believe him because he was so cute. My son Dylan is exactly the same.

I was sort of fine in Wellington until I was about 12 and then I realised that it was a sleepy backwater. Not a lot was going to happen to me if I didn't get out of there. Our quality of life was better in terms of no longer living in a cramped council flat and hearing the neighbours' rows through the walls but my Mum was often lonely because she'd left behind her clan, her tribe. My Dad had a sister, Beryl, who he didn't particularly get along with. There was also his domineering mother, so he was happy to move away. But my Mum left her roots behind. My Dad was like me. We are tumbleweed with no root system. I can shed people like a snake sheds a skin.

In Wellington, I felt like an outsider. Looking back, I remember having a rather lonely childhood once we'd moved to Shropshire. When we moved to Wellington, we moved onto a new-build housing estate. Half the houses weren't finished and all the gardens were mud. The workmen's yard was still at the end of the estate, all chained up, with loads of tractors and heavy machinery. The workmen would come onto the site every day and literally finish the estate around us. We'd climb over the gates at night to play with the cement mixer and climb over the tractors. I remember my brother having lots of friends. There were loads of boys in the street so straight away Gary had someone to play with. I was quite the Tomboy so would hang with them a lot, but there weren't many other girls there my age so there wasn't anyone for me to make friends with. It was way before the days of play dates and people coming home for tea. I used to come home from school and be on my own in my room, playing with my dolls and creating my own fantasies. We lived on the outskirts of Admaston, which back then was very rural. I'd walk down the Admaston road and there'd be ponds and trees and it would be very pretty. But I would often be on my own, or just with the dog. It seemed like everyone else had somewhere to go or someone to be with but I didn't.

It has definitely left a mark on me. Now I have children, I get quite upset if I hear there's a party going on and my kid isn't invited. It pushes that button in me that I was the kid that wasn't invited or I was the kid that didn't know what was going on. I lacked self-confidence and was often very worried. One day, at St Patrick's, I finally plucked up the courage to ask a girl from school to come round on a Saturday morning. She'd have to get the bus from wherever she lived. It was all arranged but she didn't turn up. Not only that, she didn't phone to tell me. I went to the bus stop to meet her but she didn't arrive. And I waited an hour for the next bus, just in case she'd been late, but she didn't come then either. It was heartbreaking. Her family didn't phone to explain her absence. I felt crushed. It's these silly little things in life that knock your confidence.

It's only since I've had my own children that I've made some sense of what my Mum's life was like. Her generation didn't have the choices that we now have. She hadn't really earned her own money so she was very dependent on Dad. She married very young and was 21 when she had me. My Mum was a Pools clerk when she was in her late teens, which had led to a brief, exciting career as a singer; she was a Littlewoods Songster. The Littlewoods Songsters were a big choir a bit like the Vernon Girls, who were a smaller singing group from Vernon's Pools Company.

Mum had this fantastic glittering moment. She was on aeroplanes going out to Ireland and flying around the UK. They did a Royal Command Performance and they were regularly in London and on TV. Then she married Dad. She was just making her way to the front row of the choir but got pregnant with me and so got pushed to the back to hide her bump. After that she was stuck at home with two kids. She never appeared to regret that, in as much as she would have died for us, she adored us. But as I got older, I also sensed her frustration over something that had slipped through her fingers of what life could have been like. She never mentioned it negatively, not even in any difficult moments of anger or confrontation that all families have: 'What I gave up for my kids!' But I know she must have thought about it because I'm cut from the same cloth. I'm a performer too, it's in the gene pool. There's tons of music in my family. On my Mum's side of my family, we had cousins in Canada who were singers on the cruise ships. My Dad was a great pianist, a semi-pro, who played in the clubs. He was classically trained at the Liverpool School of Music. He was a huge opera and jazz fan, which of course, when I was young, drove me nuts as it blared out of the stereo. My Dad was passionate about his music and it was always played very, very, loud. We played Nessun Dorma really fucking loud at his funeral. He had a massive record collection ranging from The Beatles, The Stones and Dusty Springfield to all of the great black artists of the time like Ella Fitzgerald, Dinah Washington, Louis Armstrong, Earl Garner and The Motown Story. Every Sunday he'd play Tchaikovsky's 1812 Overture so loud that my Mum's wall brasses used to fall to the floor. It was the '70s and by now interior design involved brasses on the walls and a copper hood over the fireplace. On the living room wall we had a brass bugle. In the morning he used to come in with this fucking bugle and play Reveille in your ear to wake you up; when you are a sulky, moody teenager, you wanted to shove it right up his arse.

My Dad was a massive personality and it was reflected in his music. I was raised on big voices like Barbra Streisand, Shirley Bassey, Tom Jones and Maria Callas. That's why I sing so big and loud. I don't know if I was physically meant to do that, but I made myself do it because I equated a great voice with a big voice: you have to give it large otherwise you are not a good singer. That's what I thought, that's what formed me. I did all my singing into a hairbrush in the mirror. I used to put all my Dad's records on and sing along or get my brother's Rod Stewart and The Faces albums. My brother could hold a tune too. He's no virtuoso or anything but he can pick things out on the piano or guitar and hum along.

Once Gary and I came along our parents put their dreams aside and settled for a more conventional life. They always put us first. I'm the only one in the family that went on to be famous through music, but it runs in our blood.

I passed my 11-plus at the local Catholic school. I remember those stats to this day. The C of E junior across the road from St Patrick's had four pupils fail out of a class of 30. Four kids in my class of 30 passed it. I finished my 11-plus so quickly that I was really worried that I'd done something wrong. I kept leafing through the paper again and again because everyone was going really slowly and I just flew through it.

After the results came to the school, a boy called Patrick McTiernan and me were asked to bring our parents in with us one day. We were invited into the headmaster's office, and I thought: 'Oh my God, it was a disaster, I am officially stupid.'

He spoke to the assembled adults: 'You've got university material here.' The two of us had sailed through the exam and got an incredibly high percentage right. Academically speaking, it was my high-water mark and I never did it again. It was a fluke. I'm really good at the process of elimination, at multiple choice stuff, which is why I do okay on TV quiz shows, but I don't really know anything in depth. Patrick on the other hand had started building TVs as a hobby at age 11!

Soon after, I found myself at a snotty girls' grammar school, where I was a misfit for the next eight years. I was always on the outside looking in. Everybody else seemed to be doing well in their various subjects but I was forever struggling with my maths. I was pretty good at English and drama, as well as singing, but I wasn't exactly egghead of the year.

My father was bursting with pride that I'd earned a place at Wellington Girls' High School. We'd gone from council flats in Liverpool to the local grammar school in the space of a few years. My brother was very bright and also passed his 11-plus. He went to the boys' grammar school.

Miss Barnes, the headmistress at Wellington Girls' High School, was a scientist and mathematician and so the school had a bias towards those subjects. I did better in the creative arts. I was encouraged into the drama club and I wasn't bad at art. I was also pretty good in the choir. The arts at my school however were viewed more as a hobby. They were not skills you forged a career out of. The clever girls were studying geography, maths, physics, chemistry and biology. We had lots of Oxbridge graduates. I was in the wrong school really. I suppose if I was young now and my parents had been a bit wealthier they'd have probably sent me to a stage school. But here I was in this highly academic school, a fish out of water who'd had a lucky day on her 11-plus. To deflect from my bewilderment I became the class clown. I spent a lot of time standing outside the class in disgrace. If Miss Barnes was patrolling the corridors I did my best to flatten up against the wall and become invisible. Being very skinny I think I actually managed it a few times. Our maths teacher, Mrs Price, could barely hide her contempt for me. It was her sport to humiliate me. Her favourite pastime was to ask me to explain to the class equations that she knew damn well I did not understand. As I stammered and flushed and squirmed she would pronounce that 'if you can't answer this question, you do not deserve a place in this school.' That is an absolutely accurate quote from 40 years ago. It's seared into my brain. As far as Mrs Price was concerned, I did not deserve my place at that school.

We had double maths on a Tuesday and I would develop a chronic and very real stomach ache every Monday evening. I remember the terror and very real nausea to this day, such is the horror of the memory.

I had some good times and a lot of bad times at school. At times I was reasonably popular but I was also scorned, bullied and ostracized. I was frequently overlooked and only very occasionally was I praised. So I have very mixed memories of the high school. And yes, I did hope that every miserable cow that ever gave me a hard time there was green with envy when they saw me on Top Of The Pops. Kiss my skinny white ass Mrs Price!

Oddly enough I did respond quite well to the strict routine of grammar school. I like to know where I'm going and what I'm doing. It doesn't sound very rock and roll does it? I was there for the eight years because I had to re-sit my A levels, which I'll tell you more about later. My favourite teacher was Mrs Pilkington, head of English, who encouraged my drama work and my appreciation of English literature. She gave me some confidence and I did well in those subjects. But despite my bravura and show-off personality, I had no true self-confidence. I could very easily be thrown and doubt myself.

When I became famous I felt, as they say in psycho-babble, 'validated'. The trouble is that when you lose that success you no longer feel valid any more. I am sure that I am broken in some way like a butterfly on a wheel. Attention always seems to temporarily fix me. Yes I know, I know, I should see a shrink. I did and it didn't work! When I left that school I didn't know what to do because I hadn't got good enough grades to go to university. I had harboured dreams of becoming a journalist because I'd watched All The President's Men and Lou Grant, but I did not secure a place at college because I flunked my exams.

Until that point, I'd also been something of a wallflower. I was 17-and-a-half before I got my first proper boyfriend. I'd had massive crushes and probably the odd fumble, but I was still new to romance and slightly awkward-looking. I was very, very skinny and I had bright red hair and wore glasses. I also still had the buckteeth – they weren't fixed until I got my brace – so I didn't exactly have boys following me in a line down the road. I was always the ugly friend of a prettier girl. Finally, when I reached 17-and-a-half, I met a boy called Martin at Tiffany's Disco, in Shrewsbury, the metropolis of Shropshire! We started dating and I slept with him, giving him my virginity. Of course I thought we'd be together forever! I was so in love with him. What I didn't know was that he was always sleeping with other people, too. He was a real Jack the Lad around Shrewsbury and very generous with his skill set. We've gone on to reconnect down the years and he knows he broke my heart, though I went on to have the last laugh. At the time, he meant everything to me. I took it really, really hard when it ended. I've always taken rejection very badly. For me to care enough to give someone my cherry and for him to go: 'fine, I've had that, I'm off….' well, it was tough. I know it happens, it's a classic story, but it really, really devastated me. I was in the lower sixth at school and I was right in the middle of my A Levels.

My Mum was amazing after it happened. I'll never forget it. When I told her, she opened her packet of cigarettes and handed them to me. I looked at her nervously. She looked straight back and said: 'You think I don't know you've been stealing my fags?' We both lit one up. It was a really important moment, we just bonded, you know, she could feel my pain.

She said: 'You slept with him, didn't you?' She was wonderful. I'd gone on the pill, so that I'd be safe and I told her every detail. I didn't have to hide anything from my Mum. My Dad came home and said: 'Why is she smoking?' and my Mum glowered at him and snapped: 'Oh shut up, Kenny.'

Both of my parents were very understanding about it. They knew I was a good girl and they knew I was hurting. They had liked Martin a lot. He was a charming, handsome boy. He charmed everybody, especially me.

Some girls were 'doing it' in my school at around age 13 and 14. I'd had a few necking sessions and played around but I was very cautious about who I finally did it with. It was a big deal to me. The loss of my boyfriend wasn't the only painful thing to happen. At that time, I thought Wellington was the most boring place in the world. I felt as though I might die if I stayed there. I was looking forward to going to college, just to get away. I expect most teenagers are like that. They grow bored in their hometown and want to break free.

Anyway, my Dad came home one night and said he had something to tell us. Dad used to do really awful jokes. On that particular evening, he did this awful sketch where he drew a really bad cake. He kept pointing to the cake telling me to guess what it meant. He was saying: 'It's intact, what does that mean, the cake's still intact.' He kept pointing at it and doing these big gesticulations. 'It's a place name. It's where we're moving. We're moving to…' and he'd point at the cake. Gary and I were flummoxed: 'What, what, what?' What are you getting at?'

He carried on with the charade, determined that we'd guess. 'We're moving to…..' then he'd point at the cake again, 'we're moving to…. None Eaten – Geddit?…..' We didn't.

'We're moving to Nuneaton.' It was the worst sketch ever. The news hung heavy in the air. It was awful. I just went: 'We're moving?' A look of horror spread across my face. It was a lead balloon moment.

Dad said: 'I've got a new job, we're going to be moving. We'll go after you've finished your A Levels.'

I was really devastated because although I thought Wellington was a boring shithole and Martin had broken my heart, the last thing I wanted to do was move somewhere else. My world was there. Even though I was unfulfilled in Wellington, there was safety and familiarity. I was worried about what would happen to me and besides, where in God's name was Nuneaton?

A broken heart and the thought of moving to a new home wrecked my A Levels completely and my grades weren't good enough for me to go to university. My parents needed to move but I was persuaded by the headmaster to stay on for another year and re-sit my exams.

The school had by now become a Co-Ed Sixth Form College and Miss Barnes had retired. It was a desperate time. All my friends had gone to uni and so I found myself in the same class as the kids who'd been in the year below when I had been a prefect. They loved it: 'Alright Decker, we've got you now.' I'd been a tad bossy, shall we say, with the power of the prefect's blue tie bestowed upon me. Being a prefect had brought out my inner jobsworth. We could give out order marks if we caught a pupil running in the corridor, or heaven forbid, scraping the remains of their lunch into the wrong waste bin.

Dad arranged for me to live with one of his work friends while I re-sat my final year of A Levels.

The guy was a former colleague of Dad's who basically couldn't stand his wife. The wife used to bend my Mum's ear endlessly. She would always be in the kitchen moaning. You know those people who don't seem to need to draw breath, who seem to have gills instead of lungs, who NEVER think you might have stuff to do other than listen to their tedious bloody life-story? Well she was one of those. She could talk a glass eye to sleep. I ended up living in their box room while I stayed on to re-sit my exams.

Life was pretty grim. I was living with an unhappy couple. Their marriage was in tatters. I retreated to my box room, alone, each evening. It was miserable. School was weird as there was nobody there that I knew. I was still getting over being dumped by my boyfriend.

I was a big fat loser who'd failed her exams and I was stuck in a horrible, shitty little room living with two people who couldn't stand each other. I just wanted to kill myself. I went to see the headmaster and told him I wanted to drop out. I said I couldn't carry on. He was a wonderful man and his eyes met mine with compassion and understanding. He said: 'Don't make a decision when you're feeling this low.' He told me I was a bright girl and that I should take my exams again. He told me I'd get my rewards if I just hung on in there. I wanted to be a journalist but I didn't have the emotional resources to support myself on my own at that age.

I was broken-hearted, my parents had moved away, my friends had gone and I was stuck with the couple from hell. I had no idea what to do next. I'd ask myself: 'Is this it? Is there a world after school? After this chaos?' I didn't know where to be or what time to be there. Eventually, I could stand it no longer and I moved to Nuneaton to join my parents and brother. I was glad to be back home, though Nuneaton was even worse than Wellington. I started working in a coffee shop. I didn't know what I was going to do with myself and I was just drifting, drifting, drifting. I had no qualifications so I thought I was looking at a dead-end life where I would just pay the rent and work in some shit shop. I got very depressed.

My parents moved from the not-very-exciting little town that I'd grown accustomed to during 10 crucial years of my life to a place where I felt totally alienated. Nearly all of my school friends had passed their exams and moved off to exciting new lives in various universities around the country. I was high and dry.

I lived in Nuneaton for about nine months and worked in a local coffee bar. Then my dad got me a job in a computer bureau. It was the pits. We sat at these funny little desks with small sort-of-typewriters and had to enter data. I was rubbish at it. I used to sit there and I would feel a hot flush of embarrassment rising up because I genuinely didn't know what I was doing. No matter how many times it was explained to me I kept having to ask the other girls what to do. Finally, the manager said to my Dad he couldn't keep me on. Thank God.

My life was drifting and I really didn't know what to do. My Dad came to the rescue again, bless him, he was always trying to help.

He had been in touch with my Uncle Roy, my Auntie Marie's first husband. Marie is Mum's older sister. Mum wasn't Roy's biggest fan. The fact that he had walked out on Marie and four kids meant Mum refused to speak to him ever again.

She didn't even go to his funeral. Roy had married again and had a little girl called Fleur. He was living in Holland and offered to let me go and stay with him and work as an au pair. It meant the opportunity to go and live in another country, which was so exciting! For about 10 months I stayed with him and his family in Eindhoven, Holland. I was wrong about Eindhoven being exciting. It was ridiculously clean but it was also a bit dull. Most of the population worked for Phillips. It was nicknamed the city of Gloeilampen or . . . lightbulbs. It was like a Dutch Milton Keynes.

I helped out looking after Fleur while working in local bars. I used to speak some Dutch but I've forgotten most of it. I can still swear in Dutch though, which is quite handy.

My uncle's second wife fascinated me. She was basically a courtesan hooking up with the next connected, wealthy man as the present one outlived his use. I wish I were that ruthless. She always seemed to get nice clothes and cars. I had started working in a bar in 's-Hertogenbosch outside of Eindhoven and was not doing as much au pair work as the wife would've liked. That impacted on her ability to shag a local antiques dealer. So I had to be replaced by someone who could mind the baby a bit more often.

I had a fling with a Frenchman while I was over there, which got me over the Martin thing. I didn't want to go back to their house so I took a room over the bar. I remember my uncle Roy shouting at me and calling me an ingrate. I wasn't ungrateful. I was just trying to live my young life. Anyway, the bar belonged to the wife's brother so she moaned at him and he sent me back to Eindhoven.

Once again I did not have the confidence to rise above everything that was going on so I retreated back to Nuneaton. It wasn't my last visit to the area, however. In a classic example of six degrees of separation, I found myself recording near to 's-Hertogenbosch when we made Rage, our second album. We found ourselves in a studio in Holland just outside the town; though I wasn't tempted to look up Uncle Roy.

I think those months in and around 's-Hertogenbosch were among the many times in my life when I've just have to dig deep, keep calm and carry on. That has happened on so many occasions. When the chips are down, I don't have any great brainstorm ideas, I just have to keep going. I'm quite risk-averse. I never go: 'You know what, this is shit, I'll go and backpack around the world.' I never do it.

To me, people who go backpacking are terrifying. I can't imagine anything more frightening. You can't speak the language, what if you get diarrhoea? There are critters that can kill you! A friend of mine, one of my bass players, went across Africa with his wife. He had a growth on his neck when he got home and ended up in a medical journal because things were growing in his neck! Why would you want to put yourself through that?

The Lacquered Knacker

After returning to Nuneaton, I found myself continuing to drift. I couldn't settle there, it didn't feel like home. Again I got a job in a coffee bar but after 10 months I went back to Shropshire and stayed with Melanie, an old school friend, in Ironbridge. She was in an amateur dramatics company in another town not far away called Bridgnorth. We'd been close at school and her mum had fostered kids, so she was used to taking in waifs and strays. She said I could go and stay with her. So I moved to Ironbridge. I too got involved with am-dram at The Bridgnorth Theatre On The Steps. At first, I helped behind the scenes, painting things or serving in the theatre bar. At last I felt there was a world where I might belong. I loved the atmosphere of the stage, even in that small town theatre, the excitement and stress of putting on a show was thrilling. Then I was promoted from helpful grunt to cast member! I ended up playing The Cat in Pinocchio. I actually got a good review in the local newspaper The Shropshire Star. The theatre was great fun. Mel had been attracted to it after meeting a guy in the local pub, The Golden Ball, or The Lacquered Knacker, as it was known in Ironbridge, he was one of the big enthusiasts at Theatre On The Steps and she was a big enthusiast of his! A romance was afoot.

The Theatre On The Steps was a great little venue and still is. Most of the time, I was perfectly happy being a grunt. The theatre was very reliant on volunteers to keep it all going, so it worked out perfectly for me. I still like the fact that volunteers are the backbone of places like that. Even though I went on to become a singer and the cherry on the top of a musical cake, I really liked the fact that in those early days I could just go along and be part of the crew. It served me well. Finally I had a sense of belonging. Mel had done really well in her A Levels and had got a place at Lanchester University in Coventry but got very homesick, so she left and came home to Ironbridge .We were both unemployed and got sent by the DHSS on a YTS scheme to work at The Ironbridge Gorge Museum.

We were on the art team. It was really cool. They were SO arty and bohemian I was very impressed. We were making these to-scale replicas of The Gorge and the pig iron works, showing the history of the area in the Industrial Revolution and how they smelted metal. Mel got the job of putting detail on the little worker figures. I was charged with making tiny bricks. There were hundreds of the little buggers.

One day we were told that Prince Charles was going to pay a visit to open the new section we were working on. Within a week Ironbridge reeked of fresh paint. Every single wrought iron railing in Ironbridge was gleaming and shiny black. The Royal family must think the whole world smells of fresh paint because everywhere is made over just before they arrive. Hanging baskets were hung. Flowerbeds were filled. Bunting was tied to lampposts. I had to go and clean up the local graveyard with the refuse team. Why did I always get the shit jobs?

Traditionally, if you're an arty person, you're quite avant-garde in your dressing. While all us museum staff had uniforms, we all dressed very jauntily. I had Dr Marten boots and I painted them different colours. It was regular paint, which was all cracked. I had dungarees, which I wore with one strap on and one strap off. All of us were paint-spattered.

At the museum, there was also a group of borstal boys. The placement gave them an opportunity to clean up their act. It was all about them doing something for the community and getting back on the straight and narrow. So, when Charles came along, all the borstal boys were suited and booted. They were dressed to impress. We all gathered in the courtyard as Charles started his speech, listening to him intently.

He went on and on and on about how wonderful the project was that we were working on and he told us that we had made a brilliant contribution. And then he turned to me and the rest of the art gang, who were wearing our scruffy art clothes, and said: 'I'd just like to say we owe an enormous debt of gratitude to those of you who have come from borstal. We are so delighted that you have taken this opportunity to put your life back on the right track.'

He'd just made the assumption that the suited and booted borstal boys were law-abiding citizens and us scruffy art lot were the ones who'd been up to no good. We didn't have any proper clothes, so we were clearly ne'er do wells. That was my first meeting with Charles, it was the first of many.

I met a lovely fella around that time. His name was Tony Howes. We quickly became involved. In fact we moved in together and got engaged. Tony was a bass player. He had gorgeous blue eyes and waist-length hair. He had such a lovely bum that drivers would mistake him for a girl from the back and honk their horns at him when he walked down the street. 'Alright, sweetheart, nice arse.' Tony would glower.

Tony's mother, Liz, owned a restaurant called Magpie House and we both worked for her and lived above it for a while. It was an awful arrangement because if we didn't leave the premises on our night off and she got busy, she would just expect us to come down and help out. We would get a right mouthful if we attempted to point out it was our night off. Liz was terrifying. She was over 6ft tall, she looked like Maria Callas and she frightened the shit out of me.

I remember we were to take a scheduled night off once and she went ape because they were a bit busy. Tony stood his ground and said we were going out. She threw dirty dishwater over us in front of customers. She was a very demanding, scary woman; just like my Nana Decker. She was tall and imposing. I was really scared of her. She relied totally on Tony. His dad had died at a young age, his sister had psychological difficulties and Liz's second husband had had a massive heart attack, was very ill and was also basically nuts. She used to make home-brewed wine and knock it all back before it had finished fermenting. Liz's moonshine was killer stuff. But it was a terrible strain on Tony to have such a needy mum. It was also, as you can imagine, not great for our relationship. After the dishwater incident we sneaked in late one night and got my stuff out of there.

We planned my escape like SAS troops and managed to get out when

Liz was out of the house. She would probably have stopped me from going because she would have been very concerned that I'd take Tony away from her. He was her rock.

Melanie's sister came to the rescue. She was living with her boyfriend, Chris, and they let me stay awhile until Tony and I found our own flat. We moved into a place in Bridgnorth's Low Town.

I had a brief spell working in a toy factory in Bridgnorth, making boomerangs that never came back. But one day I walked out for my fag break and I never came back. I was going out of my mind.

Mel and I continued to hang out and we managed to pick up some bar work. The museum placement had come to an end and Mel decided that she would like to go to art school. What a brilliant idea. I had loved the whole vibe of the art crew at the museum. We looked into it and there was a great foundation course at Shrewsbury, just up the road, at the Wakeman School Of Art.

I cobbled together a portfolio, because I could draw a bit. Somehow, I bullshitted my way into the Wakeman. This was the new me, I was going to be an art student!

On induction day, a girl plonked herself next to me. We clicked straight away. Her name was Jennie Brook and we became instant friends. Her parents were maths and science teachers and she shocked her entire family by announcing she wanted to go to art school instead of university!

Initially, I was doing an hour-and-45 minutes on the bus every day from Bridgnorth to Shrewsbury. The bus stopped in all the little villages en route and the commute nearly killed me. I was catching a bus at quarter-to-seven in the morning. So it started to make sense that I get digs in Shrewsbury. Tony was still working for his mum at the Magpie and occasionally getting a night off to play gigs as a bass player. I'd never sung at that stage; I was just his girlfriend and number one tag-along. But I remember being at the gigs and thinking: 'Cor, I'd love to be in a band.' It looked really exciting.

It made sense for me to move up to Shrewsbury, even though I was still seeing Tony. So Jennie and I started looking for a place together. Mel was happy to commute home. Jen started to see a guy who had just got

divorced. He lived almost opposite the art school. He had a big house and
he was rattling around on his own. The address was 5 Peace Cottages,
it's all gone now, it's all been redeveloped. Mike had just gone through
a messy divorce and was reliving his lost youth. He let me have the attic
room at a peppercorn rent of a fiver a week because he liked having a
house full of mad students.

He filled Peace Cottage with students. Jenny and he had a room, I
had the loft space then there were a couple of other guys sharing rooms. It
was a typical student house. It was absolutely fantastic, with dishes piled
high in the sink. Jennie got crazy about photography. That was in the
days when you had to develop your own negatives so no-one could have a
bath, a shower or a shit because Jennie was always using the bathroom as
her own darkroom. We would be hammering on the door yelling: 'Jennie,
I REALLY need the toilet!'

At first I would return to Bridgnorth at the weekends or Tony would
try to come over after the restaurant closed, but that was too knackering
for him. It was sometimes one in the morning by the time he made it
over. I began to make new college friends and there were tons of pubs
and parties to go to. I returned to Bridgnorth less and less and Tony came
to Shrewsbury less and less. Eventually the inevitable happened. I got
drunk at a party and went home with some bloke. His name was Gerry,
or was it Alan? He played guitar in a local band and I thought he was
seriously cool. He actually, cut the grass verges for the council as a day
job, but I blotted that inconvenient reality out to keep things a bit more
Serge-Gainsbourg-and-Jane-Birkin. He was actually quite a twat but I was
experiencing new situations and new people and loving it.

Because I was raised a Catholic I had to confess everything. I felt I
owed it to Tony to tell him. So I told him and he just burst into tears. I felt
awful then I found out he'd been shagging most of Bridgnorth while I was
away. Err . . .Pot Kettle Black? We tried to keep things going, but he was
very involved in his family business, trapped really. I wanted something
else. After a while we were able to become good friends. We would talk
on the phone a lot. I was delighted when he called me up to say he'd met
someone and was really happy. And they're still married now with two

beautiful boys. Sometimes you really do care about each other but it just doesn't work out. It was the wrong time.

Back at Peace Cottages, as well as locking us out of the bathroom while she developed her photographs, we also had to contend with Jennie's two dogs Pickle and Puzzle. They would crap daily beneath the dining room table, which wasn't good. I think even The Young Ones would've had trouble with the actual shit in the house. How times change. These days Jennie is so house proud that she actually criticizes my grubby tea towels. Peace Cottages was party central. We wanted for nothing.

Shrewsbury was teeming with pubs and clubs and gigs back in 1980. It was a very lively town and we had a rocking social life. Lots of great bands used to play in the clubs and the town hall. I saw The Beat, The Pretenders, The Selector and The Photo's, to name a few. In fact any up-and-coming band came to our town. It was on the circuit. We really wanted for nothing in our social life. On more than one occasion I caught a lift home, at dawn, on the milk float over the English Bridge. My Dad used to give me a little allowance. It was a fortune back then, something like £25 a month. I got a bit of a student grant and my Dad topped it up. I was always at a party. I had a job as a lifeguard at a local pool so I'd do the 7am shift in the morning before starting college at 9am. I'd always be hung over and the heat by the side of the pool was unbearable. If anybody had come close to drowning I'd have gone down with them. I wore short, red, silky Alan Partridge-type shorts with a slit up the side to show off my very Kylie-like bottom to all the swimmers. Having a whistle and a little authority brought out the natural dictator in me. Peep! 'You out!' Peep! Peep! 'Hey you! No handstands!' Oh yes, you could really take out a bad hangover on those poor sods.

I was always singing along to the radio. One day someone beside me at art school said: 'Why don't you stop annoying all of us with your constant wailing and join a band?' It's not anything I'd ever thought about even though I'd loved music my whole life. As a child I remember people remarking that almost in a heartbeat I could pick up a close harmony or the melody of a song that I had only just heard.

I've got a memory of being in our car when I was little and there was a gap between the front seats with a long skinny gear stick and a big bobble handle. This was long before seatbelts. I'd be standing between my parents' seats singing away and my Dad said: 'How do you remember all those words?' and I'd say, 'I dunno.' If you asked me to repeat them I couldn't, but if you put the song on I'd automatically know them, know the harmonies, everything.

I can sit at a piano and start picking up the melody to absolutely anything but I still can't read music. I don't know if I'm jumping on a myth, but they do say that written music is like maths and I can't do maths at all.

I loved singing, but I do think that my schooling at that girls' grammar scrambled my antenna for what I was meant to do because I'd always ignored a gift that I'd had. I'd never contemplated it as a way of making a living. It was just something I could do.

So life was great. Art school was so interesting as we covered many subjects at foundation level. Every day could be different. We'd go out and find a cobbled street in Shrewsbury and have to sit and draw the cobbles or the uneven window frames because it was such a beautiful town. I just loved it. I was so happy. I felt like I belonged. I was meeting people with alternative points of view. I felt at home. The people at art school were all misfits; and I proudly took my place alongside them. I couldn't do the suit, the conventional life. I'd finally found somewhere where I belonged and I was just so happy. My dad continued to help me out. He was such a sweetheart because he could see I'd finally found my feet.

One day at college a pal said: 'I'm going to a party at the weekend and my friend, Julian, is a guitarist and he's looking for a singer for his band. Why don't you come along? You have a really good voice.'

So I went to this house party and got introduced to Julian Ward. He had a band and was absolutely obsessed with Wilko Johnson. Julian was a Wilko double. He could play his style and do all the weird faces and the strange moves. I went along for an audition in Malcolm the drummer's garage. We were a proper garage band!

Malcolm lived just outside Leominster. It was a long drive, an

80-mile round-trip. Julian had an E-type jag which had absolutely no suspension, so you felt like you were sitting on the floor. It looked impressive but it was agony. The miles I covered in my youth were substantial because when you're brought up in a rural area you think nothing of driving 20 miles to the next place even on a pub crawl.

Initially we were a Ska band, influenced by bands like The Selector, Buster Bloodvessel, Madness and The Beat. The whole 2-Tone thing was happening. Even The Police were at it. Julian was also a fantastic reggae and ska player. His was the first band I was ever in and I owe him a lot. He gave me a way in and he had very high musical standards. We went on to have different musical styles and in the end that's why I went my own way.

Our band was called The Lazers and we wrote and recorded our own songs. We also had a covers band, The Razors, who earned more money than The Lazers. So the one bankrolled the other.

We gigged all around the Potteries, the West Midlands and North Wales. That was our catchment area. We were very busy but our gigs were in a lot of crappy pubs and working men's clubs. We'd also have to put a lot of covers in. I enjoyed the performance, that's where I cut my teeth, but I very quickly knew I did not want to be in a covers band. I wanted to be a star!

We were writing our own stuff as well. We sent some demos off to Jim Simpson, head of Brum Beat records, an independent label in Birmingham. He signed us to a short-lived deal and put us in the studio to record further demos. The band then comprised of Malcolm Wragg on drums, Alan Rowe on bass and Julian Ward on guitar with me on vocals. We made waves and got a few little radio sessions. To get a live studio session on Beacon Radio in Wolverhampton or BRMB in Birmingham was a great boost to us. It was a really exciting time.

Alan Rowe, our bass player, was funny by default. He seemed to have a constant cold which made his broad Brummie accent hard to understand. Flattened Brummie vowels through constant congestion are not easy to understand.

Often our gigs comprised of Young Farmers' Balls, which were social events rather than testicles. We would literally be playing on a flat-bed truck, which made for a very long and very thin stage. We resembled an Egyptian frieze all having to play in a long line. There was no depth to the stage and Malcolm our drummer would regularly fall off the back whilst drumming. We had to place bales of hay behind him to break his fall. I would be singing my heart out and the drums would suddenly stop, we would all look around and Malcolm would have disappeared. The set at those gigs would largely be covers.

We got to one show and the young farmers were chasing an angry pig around the barn/venue. We scattered to all corners of the barn, guitars flying in all directions: a pissed off sow is not to be messed with. Finally it was corralled in its sty. If they had have just waited for us to play Spanish Eyes, it would have left of its own accord. The organisers would often be hosing the cow shit out as we set up our gear. Oh that sickly, sweet smell of cow poo can transport me back in time. We would turn up to gigs in wellies and it would always be bloody freezing. The guys found it hard to play their guitars as their fingers seized up with cold. Most of our gigs were like that because that's the environment I grew up in.

We'd also go to The Potteries to do shows. Stoke-on-Trent wasn't that hard to get to and we'd play the arts centre where people would be drinking wine and I'm sure I saw the odd cravat.

At one young farmers' do there was a major Radio 1 DJ coming, Peter Powell, and we were on the bill. That meant that a Radio 1 DJ from London was going to get to see us! He'd think we were fantastic and we'd get a big record deal that night! It was that simple. Wait 'til he gets a load of us! Also on the bill was another local band called The Katz, fronted by Ronnie Rogers. We both did our different sets. Any thoughts of Peter Powell noticing me faded into the background. Ronnie and Twig, his sidekick, were hilarious with their onstage banter and they were also really good players. They had the crowd in the palm of their hand. I wanted to be discovered. Ron just wanted everyone to have a good time. I remember thinking he was the most handsome thing I'd ever seen. He had the pout of Michael Hutchence and the tall, gangly, raggle-taggle gypsy look of Bob Geldof, (the irony of that blend years later!) Back then

I thought both those men were gorgeous; I like a bloke not a boy, so that was fine by me. We were very attracted to each other and I went to see his band perform at a couple of local pubs.

Ronnie blew my mind on every level. I was in a long queue of girls trying to get to him. I make no bones about the fact I made a play for him. At first, I wasn't sure how to make my move because I didn't know where he lived or who he was. When we played the gig for Peter Powell, he also couldn't take his eyes off me: I don't know whether that's because he was sizing up the competition or because he felt the same way about me.

Either way, after that gig, he invited me out on a date. He took me to his youth club and we played table tennis. That was so Ronnie. My backhand was quite good so I got asked out for a second date.

We started seeing each other and it wasn't too long before we moved in together. Ronnie was charismatic, talented and great looking and I was having him in my bed and in my band! His old band mates from The Katz did not take it well, actually heckling us in the street with cries of: 'You'll regret it; she's a bitch, she's just using you.' I was in more ways than one and Ronnie loved it!

Ronnie and I were the classic case of 'opposites attract'. Ron takes his time. He's methodical and doesn't rush. I'm not. I'm the opposite. I know I said I'm risk averse in most parts of my life but I can be incredibly impulsive in my love life. When I want somebody I just go for it straight away. Or I manipulate the situation so that they think they're coming after me, but really I'm coming after them and they just don't realize it. My husband Richard, however, says that's all bollocks and if I hadn't have asked him out he would have asked me.

So life was finally on the up. I was still studying at the Wakeman, the band was going places and Ronnie and I were loved-up. Jennie had left for pastures new. She'd passed foundation after one year and was off to Sheffield Art School studying fine art. Our lives at Peace Cottage were over and so I started staying at Ronnie's flat all the time. Ronnie was sharing with a friend Danny and it was only a one-bedroom flat. Danny's bed was in the lounge and Ronnie had the bedroom. It got on Danny's nerves that I was always there. He had a girlfriend but she still lived at home and Danny liked his bachelor pad with Ronnie. All of a sudden there was a third wheel. I tried to do housework and clean the place and make tea for both of them to ingratiate myself so that he didn't mind me staying so much. But Ronnie and I both knew it couldn't last.

By now, Ronnie and I had become more serious and we started flat-hunting. We put ourselves on lots of lists and Ron got a call from the secretary of the Pengwern Boat Club. They had a loft flat over the rowing club. It was fantastic. It had a living room, bathroom, kitchen, corridor, three bedrooms and we couldn't believe it. It was £25 a month.

Ronnie was a telephone engineer. In Shrewsbury back then, you either worked for Rolls Royce or BT. Ron was BT. He earned really good money.

The Lazers, with the addition of Ron, started to get a bit of a local reputation. We acquired a manager, a guy called Nigel Hudson. He used to go into the Salop Music Centre in Shrewsbury, where Julian our guitarist was the manager. They got chatting and he came to see us perform in a pub. Nigel had his own club act as Chris Cross, singing country and western – yes both types of music. I sang all the backing vocals on his self-titled Chris Cross album. I still think that my harmonies on his version of The Gambler take some beating. It didn't seem to bother Nigel that more than a few people were disappointed when they came to a gig and discovered that it wasn't Christopher Cross, the big American star, though why they thought he would be playing in a pub in Oakengates anyway, beats me.

We got asked to appear on a regional television programme broadcast out of the Pebble Mill studios in Birmingham, appearing on Look Hear, a pop show fronted by Toyah Wilcox, who is now a good pal of mine. She had recently had her big '80s hits. I remember Pauline Black from The Selector was on the show and I hid behind a monitor and peeped at her too. I thought she was amazing but she looked rock-hard so I did not dare look right at her.

Fashion were also there. They were a new romantic band who had signed to EMI. They were THE most talked about signing but the promise never lived up to the hype. We were on the same show as all those people even though we were just a little local band.

After Ronnie joined The Lazers, he and I gradually started to take over the songwriting. I was already starting to write some lyrics for Julian's songs, which were either still ska or R'n'B. Ronnie had pop sensibilities, which really appealed to me, but we took it out of Julian's hands and of course that's when the band started to fragment.

We were always endlessly gigging, and it was hard enough to get some lazy, arrogant A and R man to cross London to see you if he'd never heard of you. So there was no way we were going to get them to come to a show in the Midlands. We had gigs in Birmingham and we tried to get them to come there or to Wolverhampton.

A Wolverhampton music journalist, and record company scout called Mike Davies, championed me. He tried hard to get people he knew in the business to come and see us play. We finally got a show at The Sir George Roby, a shithole pub in Finsbury Park, but it was on the 'credible' circuit. We had to wait for Julian to finish work at 6pm, load the gear up, and hurtle from Shrewsbury up the M1, faster than a speeding transit van had a right to, all the way to London. Not one of the companies we contacted came to see us. It was disappointing but pretty typical.

As I mentioned before The Lazers also performed in working men's clubs as The Razors, doing covers to earn money. We were the unwelcome interruption in the bingo more times than I care to remember.

Once I was singing, probably Spanish Eyes again, and an old guy in a cap handed me a piece of paper, mid-song. I smiled and kept singing, thinking it was probably a request for By The Rivers Of Babylon. I was wrong. It was actually the registration number of a car that needed to be moved. He didn't even wait for me to finish the song. He just stood and tugged at my trouser leg! But The Razors funded The Lazers' studio time, so it had to be done.

The worst attended gig we ever did was a huge pub in Birmingham as The Lazers. Nobody came at all. The landlord tried to call the gig off but we needed the fee to pay for our PA, van hire and fuel so we insisted he honour the gig. We performed to a bartender polishing glasses and not watching us and the landlord's dog spinning in circles growling and chasing his tail on the dance floor.

My college course wasn't going well. I'd started to neglect my art and they told me that if I wanted to qualify to get into university I'd have to do another year of foundation. So, Carol failed her exams again. But by then, I'd got the music bug so I dropped out a quarter of the way through year two with nothing lined up.

In 1984 after two years of slogging away with the Lazers, Ron and I left the band to start doing our own thing. With a loan of £800 from my Dad we bought a four-track studio and a fantastic new D50 keyboard with a digital programmer. You could tap in a few notes and the keyboard would play it for you. It was revolutionary in its day. It was on that instrument that Ron came up with the bass line for Heart And Soul, our first big hit. That keyboard was our baby.

I had got a job in a low-rent boutique called Fashion Flare. It sold hideous, cheap fashion on circular rails under ugly strip lighting. I earned £57 a week. If Ronnie did half-a-day overtime on a Saturday, he could earn £60. Ron really liked his job as a BT engineer so it didn't bother him at all to do a shift on a Saturday and it stopped me whining and moaning about having to work there. So I gave up Fashion Flare and got a job working as a barmaid in a pub called The Three Fishes. It was a really popular central pub and I enjoyed the contact with the regulars. It was an exciting time to work there as a movie crew were in town and they were filming A Christmas Carol, with Edward Woodward and Suzanna York. They shot a lot outside the pub and all the crew would come in for their lunch. A lot of them had just come off the latest Indiana Jones movie and they were all telling me these cool stories about Harrison Ford. I always think that the crew are the most interesting people on a movie, or a tour. They know where all the bodies are buried and they know all the stories. People like me can come and go but they work for years.

Our flat at The Pengwern was perfect for us. We had no neighbours so we could make as much noise as we liked. Initially, we had a small studio in the box room. Eventually, when we had a bit more money, we punched through the wall into the big bedroom and put the drum kit in there so we had a live room and a control room. Underneath us was a large social club. They used to let us rehearse for nothing. We got a lot out of it but so did they because we used to look after the place for them. It used to get broken into a lot until we went there but we also had some great parties. Often it was 'all back to ours' after the pub. One night a gang of us were watching a late night horror film. We had turned out all the lights to get a spooky atmosphere. At a critical part in the film and with several of us already watching the film from behind cushions, all Ronnie's home brew exploded. It took about half-an-hour for everyone to get their hearts back in their chests. I heard swearwords I did not know existed! They were gloriously happy and very funny days.

One time, however, we had our car pushed into the river. The car had been parked by the club, close to the river bank car when Ronnie and I went to bed. The next day I got up and was having my morning cuppa. I looked out of the lounge window but the car had gone.

I said: 'Where did you put the car last night Ronnie?'

He said: 'I parked it.'

'Well there's nothing there.'

So we jumped into our jeans and ran down. No car. Fuck! It's been nicked!

I looked towards the river and I saw tyre tracks and a big gouge in the bank. I shouted: 'That's where the exhaust hit, that's where it got shoved in.'

We called the police. Those were the days when there was an outside chance that the police might do something about a stolen car.

We told them that somebody had pushed our car into the river. They told us that that couldn't have happened even though there were tyre tracks to the river. The police told us that we'd obviously left the handbrake off. But Ronnie insisted he hadn't.

I said in passing, while the police were there: 'Well I hope whoever f-ing pushed it in went down with it.'

And they looked at me like I was Myra Hindley. The next thing, the frog squad were called from Birmingham and scuba divers went down looking for it. They found it then threatened to prosecute us for polluting the River Severn! We had to get it out and we'd got no money. But we had a mate with a truck and some scuba gear and he dived down, hooked a chain onto the car's bumpers and we somehow pulled it out of the river. It stayed on the riverbank for six months. It was all green and slimy and smelly. Eventually it dried out a bit and a tramp moved into it. We kept apologizing to the Pengwern committee but we didn't have the money to have it towed away to a scrap yard. After months of being patient the guys from the rowing club knocked on the door and said: 'We're terribly sorry but it's rather an eyesore, the council has been onto us and we need to push you to have it removed.' So I called my Dad and asked if he'd lend us some money again so we could pay for the car to be removed.

The tramp kept his belongings under the front seat. So I had to knock on the roof of what was now the tramp's home and say: 'I'm so sorry to disturb you, but the car's being moved in 24 hours.' And the tramp was really polite. 'Thank you so much for letting me know, I'll be on my way.' I felt so sorry for him! It was tramp heaven! He'd been living peacefully right by the river, he'd got a roof over his head, the ducks were quacking and the daffodils were growing. It was a prime location.

The car getting pushed into the river coincided with me being heckled on the street by Ronnie's former band members. You can draw your own conclusions.

Ronnie and I would write in any spare moment we had. I'd been working in a pretty cool Jeans boutique but had left after a huge row with a very unpleasant co-worker. We decided that my time would be better spent at home getting our tapes, biographies and pictures sent off to management and record companies. I became our admin!

And now I had the time, I would write constantly. I play really, REALLY bad keyboards and can block out my chord ideas for songs with the dexterity of a boxer with bound hands and gloves.

Our years at Pengwern were so important to us. That's where we wrote all of the hits. We focused on our writing for three or four years. We were just trying to get management and attention.

During those years, I almost became a TV presenter too. After our appearance on Toyah's Look Hear we got a call for me to try out as a presenter on a pilot pop show called Track One. It was a music and 'yoof' culture show. The BBC were also trialling another pilot at roughly the same time called The Oxford Road Show with Peter Powell and he got the budget. My show got canned. I was crushed at the time. I thought it was my big break to get famous, but I might never have become a singer if my career had gone down that path.

Heifers And Heartthrobs

Ronnie and I had left The Lazers and our manager Nigel Hudson had been offered a job as entertainment director for a holiday camp, so that relationship was coming to an end too. But everything happens for a reason, as they say, and in recording backing vocals for Nigel's solo album I had met and made an important connection with Simon Dawson, the sound engineer at the studio in Ross-On-Wye in Herefordshire.

Simon Dawson was the second cousin of Kingsley Ward. Kingsley owns Rockfield Studios, which was – and is – one of the best residential recording studios in the world. I can't even begin to tell you the humongous stars that have recorded there and the massive albums to come out of Rockfield. Look it up!

Simon was really dapper. He wore an Andy Capp flat hat with a neckerchief and he used to smoke roll-ups. I thought he was really snazzy. We had a brief attempt at being a couple but it was just as I met Ronnie and I knew Ronnie had my heart, even though Simon was very sweet. Simon and I became like brother and sister. I used to stay at his house in Monmouth and his mum, Angela, would bring us cocoa in bed. We would be in separate beds giggling and chatting. We were bestest roommates.

Anyway Simon thought I had a knock-out voice and played one of my tapes to Kingsley. Kingsley liked what he heard and when we had a gig at the Rotters Club, in Hereford, near to Monmouth, we invited Kingsley along. He was impressed and started giving us some studio time. He had another studio down the road called Woodside, which was a quarter of a mile from Rockfield. Kingsley had bought the mixing desk that was used to mix all of the three Star Wars soundtracks on. So we used to sit in front of the desk and think: 'Those three awesome soundtracks came out of this desk. Maybe their magic will rub off on us!'

Monmouth cast a spell over me. For a while that little town in Gwent was a hub in the international music scene with many famous and influential musicians coming and going. Kingsley was great friends with Andy Fairweather Low from Amen Corner, Nick Lowe from Rockpile, and Dave Edmunds. Like Kingsley, they were all local lads from South Wales. They had honed their respective acts in the clubs of Newport and Cardiff. Kingsley had been a keyboard player in various bands with them, before setting up Rockfield. Robert Plant lived nearby as did his guitarist Robbie Blunt and bassist Paul Martinez. Dave Charles, Ray Martinez and John David were in a signed band called Airwaves who'd had a huge hit with New Day. It was like being part of a big collective. They were the South Wales Massive.

Kingsley wore faded corduroy pants with holes in them and really ancient shoes. I don't think he ever brushed his hair. He always looked like he'd been mucking out the pigs. His eccentric brand of enthusiasm was infectious and you could hear his distinctive, high-pitched laugh from far away. On days when we thought it was all in vain Kingsley would gee us up.

Rockfield had a lot of farm land too. Kingsley once named a cow after me and another after his wife Ann. Carol and Ann shared a field happily for a few years, then I think we went to that big slaughterhouse in the sky. Kingsley said we were two of the biggest cows he knew. Only he could get away with that.

I remember going to a Rockfield Christmas party and Dave Edmunds and Robert Plant came and played. Andy Fairweather Low was there and even Shakin' Stevens. I was invited to sing back-up with that superstar line-up. I was all of a sudden hanging out with rock stars.

My dreams seemed mine for the taking. How could I fail now I was part of Kingsley's crazy world of heifers and heartthrobs?

So we were kind of in with that crowd. The drummer for Airwaves and Dave Edmunds, Dave Charles, was also an excellent sound engineer and producer. Kingsley gave us to him and Dave produced a lot of our early stuff at Woodside. That helped both us and him to develop. We went from the four-track set up at home to the 24-track on the mixing desk used for the Star Wars soundtracks. We would record at Woodside through the night until the birds were singing to make the most of our time with Dave. Back then we all smoked roll-ups. There were no 24-hour garages, so if we ran out of baccy we would get all the dog-ends out of the bin, open them up, rescue any remaining shreds of tobacco, put it in a tea strainer and re-moisten it over steam from a boiling kettle before smoking it again. I have no idea how we are all not dead.

We loved being part of that musical community around Rockfield, with guys like Robert Plant and Paul Martinez, his bass player. Paul looked like a combo of Ronnie Wood and Rod Stewart. Long, lean, rugged and tanned, he had that Captain Jack Sparrow pirate-look favoured by the old school rockers. Jewellery, a silk neck scarf, very tight pants and winkle pickers or cowboy boots were part of the look. And then there was his sort-of trendy, shaggy pineapple-shape haircut. He drove a white Rolls Royce while Kingsley had a blue one. Robbie Blunt only ever wore black; he even dyed his hair black too. Those guys had got all sorts of stories about their lives on the road and touring in the States with Robert Plant. They were all so bloody cool.

I had to be nonchalant whenever I bumped into Robert, pretending it was an everyday occurrence. We had a really nice chat in Victoria Wine once. See, Planty goes to the 'offy' just like the rest of us. Or he'd be in the pub and we'd just shoot the breeze. He was a lovely guy. I didn't actually like Led Zeppelin when I was younger so for a while, I didn't even know who he was. I just thought he was some geezer who liked a drink and a bit of a chat. I didn't know that he was a bona fide Rock God.

As well as the resident stars there would also be a steady influx of bands recording at Rockfield and they too would be in the local pubs in the evening. Simon had also been on tour as a monitor engineer for different bands and some of the crew and partners he had toured with would come down from London and stay the weekend. They were all so glamorous and well-travelled; I lapped up their tour stories of Japan and The States. Often there were stories about the different sexual skills of different nationalities of groupies: apparently American girls give the best head. Stories of the Mile High Club on long haul flights would abound.

They had all been to places I had only read about in magazines and done things that were all so glamorous and naughty. There were lots of parties and they even brought then-exotic food with them like Ciabatta bread and that awful bitter endive salad. I had my first glass of Chardonnay at that time and it was also the first time I ever saw a Stilton cake. Stilton cake was made by taking a big round of Stilton cheese and scooping out the middle before filling it with port and digging in with a spoon. The cheese started to turn to mush and you'd get drunk on cheese. It was exotic, grown-up life. We didn't run to all this in Kwik Save in Shrewsbury.

Ronnie and I were getting an education in everything and we loved every moment. More to the point, they were all in the music 'biz. We seemed to be making the right sort of friends.

Life was a constant mix of Shrewsbury and Rockfield. We'd record at Woodside and hang out at Rockfield whenever we were able to before retreating to Shrewsbury. Shrewsbury was germane. We wrote about 35+ songs during those years of living at The Pengwern and visiting Monmouth. We'd go out on Friday and Saturday nights, if we weren't in Monmouth and live it up with our mates. Then we'd work in our home studio during the week.

If we were at a loose end we'd hang out at Salop Music Centre, which at the time was down by the Town Walls. All the aspiring local musos would be in there. If you didn't want to stay at home you could just go to the local music shop and hang out, or fiddle with the keyboards and guitars. You'd get chatting to other musicians and staff and there'd be a noticeboard with people looking to recruit a band member. It was a good meeting point.

Kingsley was personally hawking our tapes around as he had signed us to a production deal so Dave and he could have part of whatever happened to us when it took off. He would also go to The States frequently and that's when he came up with the phrase 'I'm talking big here, I'm talking America.' Ronnie and I liked that so much that for the better part of 18 months, we were called Talking America. We took constant advice; Dave Charles would tell us which songs he felt were worth working on each time we brought a new batch.

We had a great little band. Ronnie would play most instruments and Dave would drum. Andy Fairweather Low often played guitar for us too and I played the occasional simple keyboard part. We borrowed the latest state of the art keyboard from Rockfield called the Jupiter Eight. I had never heard anything like it in my life. The string sounds were the most authentic around. It sounded like they'd somehow squashed an orchestra beneath the keys and it revolutionised the way our songs sounded. At home we had an analogue four-track mixing desk and an old guitar amp spring that we used as a reverb unit on my voice. I can't explain to you how important it was to us to have access to that level of equipment. We sounded pro! We sounded expensive. I wanted strings on EVERYTHING!!!

Having that kit also meant we could not stop tweaking. If you have no gear you make your decisions quickly. But if there are different options, it can take forever and Ron could tweak for Britain. I am known as 'that'll do Decker' and it's a good job because Ron would still be tweaking our demos now if I hadn't stopped him. We lived like vampires, working through the night and sleeping in the day, hiding from the sun.

We were approaching 18 months of working with Dave and Kingsley. But despite how great our excitement with each song we finished and despite all our hard work, Kingsley had not secured us a deal. There was always something not quite right about us for the record labels. No-one was biting and eventually he had exhausted all his contacts without getting a bite.

One day I was home alone at the flat, Ronnie was at work and the phone rang. It was Kingsley. He told me that he and Dave reluctantly

felt they had given as much time and energy as they could and they were
pulling out of the production deal with us, essentially withdrawing our
access to the studio. I froze, I was actually speechless. He basically said:
'Look you know we love you, we think they are all idiots not to see
how talented you are but I think I've gone as far as I can. I've spoken to
everybody I know and there was always something missing. There was
always something they weren't happy with. We will always listen to
any songs and if there's anything we hear that is a sure-fire hit of course
there's always a relationship here but we want to look at other things,
other acts.' We never heard from Dave. I put the phone down and started
to cry. Kingsley was our lifeline to the rest of the world and in the space
of a phone call that was gone. When Ronnie got home I was in floods of
tears. He was really disappointed too. We'd become so close to Dave and
Kingsley that the separation actually hurt. Ronnie handles things in a very
measured way. He's a happy, self-confident guy, who will always make
the best of his life whatever happens. Ronnie often used to say to me:
'Enjoy the journey in case we don't make the destination.'

After about a day of reflection Ronnie thought fuck 'em, we'll be OK
but I went on a terrible downer. I truly believed we were on our way to
success with Dave and Kingsley and now that was over.

Months of nothing followed. We didn't know what to do. We weren't
even in a band any more. The huge disappointment of being dropped
by Kingsley and Dave put a real strain on our relationship too because
I became pretty miserable about everything. I wasn't good at hiding my
feelings and I was depressing to live with. Ronnie suggested he could
transfer to BT Reading, so that we could be closer to London. But I
didn't see the point. It didn't feel right. I thought if we couldn't move into
London and be in the thick of it there was no point in being in another
town where we didn't know anybody. Again, I was risk averse. We knew
everybody in Shrewsbury. I was frustrated and depressed but I felt safe in
Shrewsbury and I had all my friends. I couldn't see the point of moving to
Reading just to be near to London.

A few months later I got a call from my cousin Susan whose
then-husband had a jazz/funk band called The UK Players signed to

EMI. They needed a backup singer and Susan suggested me for the gig. I desperately wanted to do it. The idea of being on a tour with a signed artist thrilled me. As I broached the subject with Ronnie, I felt seriously guilty. But he absolutely wanted me to do it. He knew I was going to explode if I didn't get some momentum in my career. He didn't begrudge it at all. Ron's a very independent person. If something doesn't go right, he won't dwell on it, he'll just move on. We didn't know what the future held for us as a writing partnership so I went off on tour and Ronnie stayed at home, still working for BT, and everything settled down for a while.

The UK Players Tour was exciting and intimidating for me. It was not my band. I was not in charge. I give my all on stage and I get lost in a performance. But that wasn't what they wanted from me. I got told off for standing out too much as a backup singer and warned that I should cool it.

There was another back-up singer called Chrissie, a very cool black girl. The style of music was jazz/funk, essentially MOBO. When the MD complained that one of us was out of tune, they believed it was me. The band had a prestigious session at Radio 1 on a day off and I kept asking when the date was because I was SO excited. But they did it without me. I called my cousin when I found out because I was utterly humiliated. She was deeply embarrassed but was not allowed to say anything to me. I tuned in to listen to the session and all the world could hear the other girl singing so far out of tune you could almost see the bend in the notes. They had made an assumption the uncool ginger white girl had to be singing jazz/funk out of tune but I was the one who was spot on. I got a flat out apology.

The tour lasted around a month. The band weren't actually very nice to me as I didn't do cocaine while they were all hoofing it down. It was the '80s after all. My abstinence made them very suspicious of me and I got quite lonely. I asked a friend years later why, after all my success, I didn't seem to be very well connected or invited to many showbiz things. She said: 'That's because you weren't in the bogs doing toot.' Apparently that was where all the cool showbiz friendships were made. I was always propping up a bar in a pub rather than being in the loos of a cool club.

When I finally did try some coke at the grand old age of 38 we spent the entire night in a toilet. It was a waste of time.

Back home in Shrewsbury the experience of the UK Players' tour kept my spirits buoyant for a while. Ronnie and I were still writing and sending tapes away but it was also okay for me to look at other things. Ronnie wanted me to be happy for my own sake, as well as his, as it took the pressure off him having to keep me happy. Looking back I can now see that he was wisely but reluctantly prepared to say 'Que Sera Sera' to whatever happened to us as a couple then, though we stayed together for 13 years. Things may have worked out differently if I had not always been so ambitious and restless.

Out of the blue, at some point in 1986, our luck changed. We got a call from a guy after I'd answered his advert. Bands and management used to put adverts in the back of the music press when looking for new recruits 'name band want backing vocalist' and then they'd hold open auditions for it. I'm sure it's much more of a closed shop these days and a record company or MD will source backing vocalists and the ancillary musicians. But back then you'd put an advert out and see who rocked up.

The guy who called was a man named David Massey, who managed Wang Chung, who were then massive. He phoned me up and said: 'Hi, I got your tape, you have a great voice. I manage Wang Chung.' My heart stopped and I thought 'Oh My God! I'm going to sing with Wang Chung.'

Dave carried on: 'Now look, I've filled the position with. . . .' My heart sank.

But he continued: 'But my mother, Marion Massey, manages Lulu. Lulu is going out on tour and there's a space for a backing vocalist. I really like your voice and I think you'd benefit from the experience.' No offence to Lulu but it wasn't exactly the sort of rock'n'roll road trip that I was looking for.

I tried to feign interest and gratitude but I was already tuning out of the conversation. He then went on to say: 'I really like that song Valentine. You need to write more like that, it shows the power in your voice, the passion you have as a singer.'

And so began our telephone friendship with David Massey, who went on to be, and still is, a luminary figure in the record business, heading up several huge labels. There was never a formal arrangement between us, but he used to phone us up regularly and say: 'How's it going?' David said we could call him any time, ask him for any advice, he was a mentor and pal. Frustratingly, once again, we were intriguing someone of influence but there was something missing that prevented him from carrying it forward full-time. We needed someone like David plugging our tapes and taking meetings with the record labels because without that we couldn't get through the door.

David used to say: 'Always send me your songs.' So we'd send him more stuff and he'd say: 'It's not Valentine.'

I signed up to do Lulu's tour and Ronnie, bless him, drove me all the way to Surrey, where she was rehearsing. He patiently waited in the car for hours and the whole thing was very cabaret, not my scene at all, but it was work and she was Lulu! That was back in the days long before Take That had made her cool again. A few days later I got a call from Marion to thank me but sadly Lulu had pulled the tour after being offered the role of Pauline Mole in The Growing Pains Of Adrian Mole. She'd been due to start filming soon for a 1987 release date.

I continued answering other ads and got another audition for the popular jazz/funk combo Shakatak. For that one, my Mum drove me all the way down to London. I couldn't drive until I was 33; I was either too broke for lessons or, later, being driven in a limo.

My mother, bless her, was a very timid driver. We drove to London and she was terrified of all the traffic. There we were going round Piccadilly Circus. We were stuck behind all this traffic and got into a jam behind a taxi. The lights didn't seem to be changing and we just got marooned behind this cab for what felt like an age. My audition slot was looming ever closer and I thought I was going to be late. I started panicking because we just couldn't move. And then the guy in the cab in front of us got out with a sandwich in his hand. He walked towards us and knocked on Mum's window. 'You're in the taxi rank, love,' he said, laughing. We'd been sat there for 10 minutes. Fools. But we couldn't see over the height of the taxi. There were all these big fat cabbies having their lunch. Finally I got to the Shakatak audition, though I didn't get it.

I will never forget lead singer Jill Sinclair personally phoning me up. I nearly passed out when she did as I thought I had the gig. But alas she said: 'You have a wonderful voice, but we've picked somebody different. I just want to tell you that you're not quite right for us but you're fab.' It was not the news I wanted to hear but Jill was remarkably genuine for making the call herself and not leaving it to her PA.

It felt like Groundhog Day and I was crestfallen again that I wasn't quite right. But these things happen for a reason; maybe if I had got the gig I'd have ended up as a backing vocalist. Funnily enough I bumped into Shakatak for the first time since then last year on The Gabi Roslin Show. I said: 'Do you remember my auditioning for you?' And they laughed: 'We sure do and we should have given you the gig!'

David Massey continued to keep in touch with us. He always said Valentine was the song. I asked him: 'Why won't you manage me?' But he said he hadn't got the time. I was always in these situations with people telling me they thought I was great but they didn't want to get completely involved with me. That just taps into my personal insecurities and my big fear of rejection. I thought: 'If I'm so great, why don't you want to take that further step with me?' But they never did. David Massey didn't want to take the next step, Kingsley decided to stop, record companies shillied and shallied over our tapes but always eventually decided no; people I auditioned for told me I had a fabulous voice but I wasn't quite what they wanted. When was I going to catch a fucking break? I was 25 by now. I kept going because I knew I had something and that failure was not an option. I had looked over the edge of the precipice into a life of dead end, dull jobs. There was no alternative.

I was always trawling through the music papers and naivety is a wonderful thing. If I could give any young musician advice it would be: screw it, just do it. So I'm looking through the back pages of the Melody Maker or NME, I forget which, and there was a touring advert saying Harvey Goldsmith Proudly Presents The Pretenders. I just adored The Pretenders. I thought Chrissie Hynde was fantastic. I so related to her tomboy image.

I wrote to Harvey Goldsmith and sent him a demo tape, saying: 'Dear Mr Goldsmith, next time you are looking for a support act for one of your big tours , look no further than us, we are fab, here's a tape and a picture showing you how fab we are.'

I didn't know anything about record company buy-ons back then. Labels pay a fortune to buy on to a tour. You pay the headline act for the privilege of the exposure you will get as their opening act. A few years later our label paid £25,000 for us to support Bryan Adams across Europe. However, I didn't know about any of that then. I just knew that Harvey Goldsmith Enterprises was huge and he was the promoter behind the stars of the day, not to mention Live Aid.

Harvey was just starting a management arm to his empire and our tape got passed along to Chris Cook, who was working for Harvey on the fledgling management side. We got a call from Chris: 'I've got your tape.' I thought he was going to say: 'And you're going on tour with The Pretenders!' But no.

He said: 'I really like your voice and stuff. I'd like to put you in a studio, get some more recording done, do you want to come down and meet?' Hell yes!

My parents took us and we stayed at The Bonnington Hotel on Southampton Row. I thought it was The Ritz. Over the tannoy, they said: 'Would Miss Carol Decker please come to the main desk please.' The fact that there had been a tannoy announcement of my name in a London hotel meant I was already a star! I was giddy with excitement. So we hopped in a cab to meet Chris Cooke. He said he thought we were great and he wanted to start working with us. He told us that he ran Harvey's management company but as far as Ronnie and I were concerned, Harvey Goldsmith had just taken us under his wing. We did get to meet him that day and also shook his hand. Chris was going to introduce us to the next level of producers, musicians, movers and shakers so that we could refine what we were doing. It was all starting to fire up again. It was more than we'd dared to hope for.

A couple of weeks went by and Chris phoned up again. He told us he'd left Harvey Goldsmith to set up his own management company. I was just gutted because, you know, who didn't know Harvey Goldsmith? He had worked with everyone: Paul McCartney, Queen and The Who, U2. The list was endless. He had helped to organise Live Aid in the space of a few weeks. Bob Geldof and Midge Ure had the idea and the song but I'm pretty sure when the biggest stars of the day learned that Harvey Goldsmith was on board to pull the production together, they all jumped on board. That would have inspired huge confidence in them.

Harvey was The Man. And our connection with him had gone. He was the most influential promoter in the world. We didn't know why Chris left, he was vague about having his own ideas and wanting to do things differently. All of a sudden Harvey didn't want to do artist management at all, we were told. He'd had a change of heart. It came as a shock to Ronnie and I to learn that.

Chris set up his own company called MI5 Management. By now I was 26 and positively geriatric. A very abrasive and terminally hip stylist called Jackie Castellano was drafted in to make us over and we were booked to do our first proper photo shoot.

Jackie had been styling and 'sort of' managing Hugh Cornwell, of The Stranglers. She had quite a reputation for being tough. I remember Jackie being very concerned about my age and literally peering at my skin from an inch away then announcing I could shave off a couple of years in press releases as I looked a bit younger than I was. She told me, unflatteringly: 'Crows' feet will be coming very soon.'

Jackie was rather imperious about the effort it was going to take to get Ronnie and I into shape as we were country hicks. She insisted on a hefty monthly retainer and said that under no circumstances would she take public transport; she took cabs everywhere and billed them back to us on top of her retainer. Chris was fronting all of the outlay and we were quite intimidated by her and would probably have worn anything she suggested out of pure fear.

All the same, I have to say we looked stunning in our first proper shoot. Ronnie was so tall, dark and handsome and I was a fox in a see-through white lace Issey Miyake trouser suit. She did a great job. When you get a really good stylist, they see you objectively and completely differently to how you see yourself. With the exception of the occasional disaster, I have learned so much from cutting-edge makeup artists and stylists. I know how to put myself together.

So Chris then became our lifeline to the London scene. We were still living in Shrewsbury. Chris had rented a four-storey house as offices, with a couple of flats upstairs on Meard St, yes, shit street, just off Wardour Street, in Soho. It was the balls! We could stay there any time we liked when we were in the middle of town. Chris took on a PA called Teresa Wareing, a funny, smart Scouser, and we remain great friends to this day. By now, Chris had introduced us to Tim Burgess, our drummer, and Taj Wyzgowski, who became our guitarist. They both lived in London so when we were demoing in studios they were part of the team.

Soho has always been a vibrant and lively part of London. But back then it wasn't slick and gentrified as it is now. There were more sex clubs and peep shows. One night, a bit well-oiled, we could not resist a sign over a peep show club that read: 'Naked Girls 50p'. We thought that was a bargain. Ronnie and I were in the peep booth and had to put 50p in a slot machine: Ta da. A window opened and there was a very bored naked young lady lying with her legs open. There was a knock on our door and a Fagin-like voice croaked 'room for one more?' EEEUURRRRGGGH!!!!!! I think we screamed and ran away.

Chris knew a lot of people and the first thing he secured for us was a publishing deal with MCA of £5,000. We couldn't believe it. Based on this humongous sum of money Ronnie decided to take the plunge and quit his job at BT. He didn't tell his dad for another six months though, and when he did Ron Snr. was not happy. BT offered well-paid work and he thought Ronnie was being really irresponsible. Naturally he came round later.

The deal with MCA had us signing over a lot of the songs that would end up on Bridge Of Spies: Sex Talk, Valentine, Monkey House, Friends Like These, Maggie, Heart & Soul, and China In Your Hand had yet to be written. We bought some more equipment and improved the studio back home.

Chris also introduced us to a new producer, Andy Piercy, from After

The Fire, who'd had a deal, some radio play and had also supported Queen on tour. Andy was trying to branch out as a producer so it suited us all to go into the studio together. Tim was on drums, Taj on guitar and we met the most fantastic keyboard player, Reg Webb. Reg was completely blind and yet somehow managed to get the Tube with his huge keyboard in tow. He was as independent as any jobbing musician. Reg had the most incredible feel on keyboards and laid down a few tracks for us, including fabulous parts on Maggie, which was my clumsy attempt at political posturing.

We used to play jokes on him in the pub after a day's recording. We'd all have drink, a fag and some crisps. Then we'd make it a competition to see who could silently nick Reg's crisps while the rest of us kept him talking.

Amongst the new studio gear we bought was a Roland JX3P keyboard with a built-in sequencer. That meant we could programme in the musical notes and create a pattern that the computer could keep playing in sequence. Ronnie spent hours reading the manual and acquainting himself with his new toy. In contrast, I've always been totally useless with studio gear and am immediately baffled by the tech info. I assume it's like maths and I am too stupid to understand it, plus I severely lack patience. For example, Ronnie enjoyed understanding how a telephone worked. I just needed it to work and if it didn't, I'd throw it out of the window!

Eventually Ronnie came up with a sequenced bass line that went on to become the bass lick for Heart And Soul. We started working the song up. I had recently been on holiday with my parents to Marbella, but Ronnie couldn't come and I had really missed him. I had sat at the edge of the ocean as the sun went down, and melodramatically looking out to sea I came up with the lyric for the first verse: 'More than an ocean keeps us apart, I feel a tearing in half of my heart'. Together we found the verse chords we needed and pretty much wrote the whole thing over a couple of days. When Andy Piercy heard the track he really liked it but thought it needed something percussive running through it as it was pretty mournful, dreamy and linear. He started sort-of grunting and doing vocal beat box to illustrate the movement he was hearing. Instead of conventional percussion I came up with percussive words: I just started throwing words into the holes in the rhythm to fill the song.

'Something in the moonlight catches my eye, the shadow of a lover goes dancing by…' It is still the song that I am most proud of as a songwriter. It is unique.

So on we went again, meeting up with Andy, refining our songs, trying to catch a break. Although we were often close, the ever-elusive deal was not on offer. After another year slipped by, our MCA publishing deal was up for renewal. Not only did they pass on renewing it, but they gave us our songs back for nothing. I remember very clearly being incredibly upset once again. I actually felt insulted that they thought so little of the songs they didn't even want to keep them. I didn't realise how lucky we were to get them back.

The MCA money ran out and Ronnie and I were both signing on. We were so skint that Chris or my Dad would pay the odd utility bill for us. Ronnie's Mum was Chief Pie and Sunday Lunch provider. We had no heating in the flat, other than one wall-mounted gas fire in the lounge that had a 50p slot. It would race through that 50p in about an hour and you couldn't feel the benefit unless you stood right in front of it – and then your jeans got too hot and burned your leg. There was also ice on the inside of our windows.

Living in a boating club we were down beside the river at the lowest point of The Quarry, the huge park in the centre of Shrewsbury. If it snowed or got icy, it was the last place to thaw out. Often it flooded too. On more than one occasion, we had to climb above the flat on the hillside, wearing our wellies with our shoes in a carrier bag. We'd get to higher, drier land, swap wellies for shoes and hide our wellies in a bush for the return journey. It was a challenge to live there at times. Recently I was invited to view our old flat by the current tenant and it had all been done up and had central heating. But I could still see the ghosts of us there. Anyway, things were getting more than a bit desperate. We really needed some funding. We really needed a record deal.

Chris had another business interest with a man who made and sold tiny pottery cottages. The guy, a private investor, had lots of money. We went to London to meet Chris and he told us he had some good news. Pottery Cottage Man wanted to invest in us. Ronnie looked dismayed and I actually shouted: 'No! We want a record deal! I want to be able to say I am on EMI or Virgin, or Polydor. I want to be on a proper record label, and we'll be on what label? Pottery Fucking Cottage Records?'

But now, of course, lots of people have deals like that. Chris was essentially crowd-funding. With the disassembling of the music business and the decline of all those record labels, lots of people are now getting private investors to fund albums and movies. Looking back, Chris was probably ahead of his time, but to us it was not the way things were done. Being on a big label had kudos. It meant you were a bona fide recording artist. I needed a big label behind me because it told the world: 'I was thought good enough to get a record deal so listen to me'. The record company label was all-important. So it was not going to work with Pottery Cottage Man. We gave him a resounding 'NO'; his pottery cottages were shit, too.

Chris stoically continued to plug our tapes and knock on doors. Finally somebody opened one by a tiny crack. Siren Records was a subsidiary label of Virgin Records and Simon Hicks was head of Artist and Repertoire. He was AKA A&R, AKA 'Um and Ah', as they were known to most musicians. He and Siren MD David Betteridge said they liked the tape: 'We'd like to see the band gig.'

The problem was there was no band. We had the guys we recorded with but that was not the same as being rehearsed up to speed. Also, we didn't gig any more so we had no show and we had no following, so who was going to turn up? Ronnie and I just had each other and the songs. So Chris had to bluff it a bit and say: 'They are focused on writing and recording in the studio at the moment and are not actually gigging, but we could showcase it for you.'

Siren agreed to pay for a big rehearsal room at Nomis Rehearsal Studios in Shepherd's Bush. Back then Nomis was a really cool rehearsal space owned by Simon Napier Bell, Wham's manager. Nomis is Simon spelled backwards, for all you pop trivia nuts.

The huge stars of the day were rehearsing in the other studios, walking the corridors and eating in catering. George Michael was there as well as Chris Rea, Simply Red and Huey Lewis & The News. I nearly fainted.

We cobbled together a band made up of musicians we'd recently met: Tim Burgess on drums, Taj Wyzgowski on guitar and a bass player from back home called Paul Jackson. The local Telford band he was in had paid to do a demo in our studio and Ronnie thought we was good, so we asked him along. We had no keyboard player however. Reg Webb had been helping out courtesy of Andy Piercy and we couldn't afford him as he was an in-demand session guy.

Taj said he had a mate Scott Firth, 'Scotty', who could came along and play keyboards. The trouble was we had no opportunity to meet him and rehearse but Taj told us not to worry. He said he'd just get a tape of the songs to him, he was really good and we'd be fine. The rest of us already knew the songs. We all arrived at Nomis good and early to routine them. Siren were due at 12 noon.

The clock struck 10am and Scotty hadn't arrived. Understandably, I was on edge. It was two hours to the most important audition of my life and the band was still incomplete. I didn't really know if Scotty would be any good. In fact, I'd never even met him and I knew nothing about him. We were still in the days before mobile phones were common so none of us could get hold of Scotty to see where the fuck he was. By the time it got to 11am, I'd become apoplectically anxious. I'd smoked all my fags and had really bad nervous diarrhoea. I was getting thinner by the second. I wanted to kill Scotty and by default also kill Taj who had recommended him. Once more a huge opportunity was about to slip through my fingers because some arsehole musician couldn't turn up on time.

At around 11.15am, Scotty breezed in, all-charmingly-Scottish, shaking hands and saying 'hi'. I did my best to conceal my black heart and keep the murderous look out of my eyes. Ronnie and Tim said we needed to quickly run through the songs, even though we only had three prepared: Sex Talk, Valentine and Monkey House. And do you know what? Scotty was bloody fantastic. He played all three without dropping a note. It later turned out he wasn't really a keyboard player. I wanted to marry him and have his babies.

Years later we worked with Scotty on a few recordings; he can play bass, guitar and keys like a dream. He's a very talented guy but on that day I did not know that and he did nearly give me a heart attack.

At 12 noon, Chris showed Simon and David into the studio. We all shook hands and made idle chit chat. Then we could no longer put off the inevitable. We had to play the songs.

We kicked off with Sex Talk. It was odd doing a showcase to three people but we all played out of our skins, it was like we were playing at Wembley Stadium. I was singing so hard I think I burst a vein in my neck. At the end of each cacophonous song, there were just three people clapping politely. It felt like falling off a cliff each time we ended a song. But that was three people more than in that pub in Birmingham all those years ago.

I could barely speak after our short set, so thank God that's all we had to do because I gave it 110 percent, as sportsmen say.

Then things unfolded just like an episode of the TV show Fame. David Betteridge looked at Simon Hicks, the A&R guy. They smiled at each other, looked at us and said: 'You've got a record deal.' We all shook on it. They said: 'It's a done deal. Fantastic. We love her. We love the songs.' We babbled a dozen thank yous.

Chris escorted them out and when the door clicked shut we screamed and bounced off the furniture. We jumped off the PA stacks and bounced off the walls, off the ceiling. I couldn't believe it. I'd never been so happy in my life. It was a stellar moment.

Chris came back in and after 10 minutes of just taking it in, he pulled out a hefty looking collection of papers. It was a management contract. We had never actually signed anything with him. It was all done on faith. He wanted us to sign it there and then. Ronnie and I felt really uncomfortable with the timing. Chris said: 'It's nothing, just sign it. If your lawyer has any issues we can take care of that, it goes in a drawer and we forget about it unless we need it.' We felt so indebted to the guy that we signed it without any immediate legal advice.

And later, against the advice of our lawyer who pointed out things

that were not as favourable as they should've been, we felt too guilty
to question the man who had stood by us and helped to finally make it
happen.

The following day, still euphoric, Ronnie and I drove back to our
flat at The Pengwern in Shrewsbury. We opened the mail that had
accumulated when we were away and amongst it was a rejection letter
from Virgin Records. They owned Siren, the label that had just offered
us a deal. I kept it and later gave it to David Betteridge when we were
at number four in the US Billboard charts. He framed it and put it in his
office loo.

Chris was able to use the fact that we were recording as a lever to get
better gigs and soon we hit the road in Europe. We had recruited Michael
Chetwood, a Shropshire-based keyboard player. Mike was a bit older
than us and had been in a line-up of Robert Plant's Band Of Joy. He had
been involved with other bands down the years who'd had record deals
and almost-but-not-quite made it. That made him cynical. He was at that
point in time the manager of the keyboard department at Salop Music. He
had set his dreams aside and was loath to give up a steady job and salary.
When we were able to tell him we had money and could offer wages if he
took the plunge with us.

The line-up was now compete: Tim Burgess on drums, Paul Jackson
on bass , Michael Chetwood on keys ,Taj Wyzgowski on lead guitar,
Ronnie on rhythm guitar and yours truly on lead vocals.

With our record company advance we bought a second hand
Mercedes 508D van and had it customized to hold the gear in the back.
We installed aeroplane seats with individual headphone sockets, none of
which ever seemed to work, just like on a real plane. We were ready to hit
the road. All we needed was a name.

Naming a band is a tricky job. Every time you have a eureka moment,
'I've got it!' – someone else will hate it. Many meetings in several pubs
were called to come up with the right world-captivating nomenclature for
our new musical ensemble. I can't remember which ideas the other boys
chucked in but everybody piped up with names. None of us could nail it.
Whoever came up with a name, at least four of the other members of the

band would say 'not a chance, I'm not being in a band called that, f- off.'

I had been back home at the flat, pottering about and catching up on the ironing. I had the TV on in the background and an episode of Star Trek was showing. It was the original series with William Shatner as Captain James T Kirk and Leonard Nimoy as Mr Spock. In the storyline of the episode Amok Time were two of Spock's Vulcan female relatives, T'pring and T'Pau. I really liked how T'Pau sounded, I couldn't get it out of my head, so in another emergency 'directors' meeting' in The Crown and Two Chairmen, in Soho, I put it to the lads: 'How about T'Pau?'

There was a silence. The band looked at me and said: 'Well that's the least shit name that anyone's come up with.' So I said: 'OK if no-one's got anything better, that's it, we need a name.' T'Pau was born.

Years later, Roy Thomas Baker managed to get me a signed picture from Leonard Nimoy. He had written the Vulcan greeting 'To Carol and T'Pau, live long and prosper.'

Although I was not a Trekky , I realised this was a very cool photo to have, but I had never gotten around to framing it and it was just propped up on my bedside table. One day I decided to have a quick dusting session in my bedroom. I sprayed my duster with furniture polish and gave the now quite dusty pic' a wipe. The dedication came clean off. There was not even an imprint or pen indentation I could go back over. I now had just a picture of Leonard Nimoy. I don't know what he signed it with but had the man never heard of a Sharpie!

Freddie Mercury Cottage

Meanwhile, back on the road, we had our new van and Jennie Brook my college pal was our roadie and tour manager. It was very unusual back then to have female crew outside of wardrobe and catering. We had two tough girls in our set up: Jennie was on the road with us and Teresa Wareing was in the office. They were like me, not your average girl. You had to be tough and single-minded in the male-dominated world of music. It didn't make me the girliest of girls so my girlfriends were few and far between.

We were heading out to play a gig on The Grosse Freiheit, a street on the The Reperbahn, in Hamburg. Our most recent demos had been played to a selection of interested, big-time producers including Nile Rogers and Roy Thomas Baker (RTB). Nile Rogers was the most amazing producer but the direction we were heading in back then was more suited to RTB. Ronnie in particular loved Queen and we both loved the four albums he'd produced with The Cars. RTB had a rock/pop pedigree as long as your arm. It was agreed he would come to Hamburg to see us play. I can't remember much about the show other than that it wasn't packed out and we were on with a few other local bands with a bit of a following. Suffice to say that RTB was sufficiently impressed to agree to record our first album.

Roy had a first-class sound engineer called Jerry Napier, who had been Neil Young's front-of-house tech for many years and was now working full-time with Roy. Part of Jerry's job was to scout good deals in studios for Roy's projects and he found a studio near Chicago called Royal Recorders. It was part of a golfing hotel complex that had been owned by Hugh Heffner. The studio ran independently of the hotel and was keen to get Roy on the résumé. All I heard when Siren told us where we were recording was 'Chicago!' Having been raised in sleepy Shropshire and having had a huge crush on those iconic American cities, it was a dream come true. I could see myself cruising round The Windy City, having Happy Hour cocktails in cool bars downtown, jogging round Lake Michigan even though I hated jogging.

We said goodbye to the fields and cows and small towns of Shropshire and flew out to Chicago O'Hare International.

We were picked up by the studio staff in a couple of vehicles and began our drive to Royal Recorders. As the tall glass shards of Chicago's gleaming sky scrapers faded into the distance, I started to get a bit worried. After a two hour drive we were in Lake Geneva Wisconsin, a small country town surrounded by fields and cows.

I had not picked up on the word 'near' Chicago. It would not be the last time I only heard what I wanted to hear! Though the fact we were miles away was probably a good job as I am not sure how much work we would have got done if we'd been in the city. We did of course have some days and evenings off, and got to shop and party in Chicago.

For the first month we had rooms in the hotel. That was really convenient as we could work as late as we wanted, then fall into bed. We got into quite a bit of trouble for stealing the golf carts, hot-wiring them and driving all over the golf course at night when we were pissed. The studio manager received a formal complaint from the hotel. We denied everything, of course. But we got our marching orders and the label had to rent two big houses a few miles away for us to stay in. They were just like the ones you see in an American sitcom with a big kitchen, big living room and a big spacious square hall with a shiny wooden floor, perfect for our new late-night game of skid-rug!

Skid-rug involved drinking a lot then, after placing the hall rug in the middle of the room, you had to back up to the far wall, sprint and launch yourself onto the rug and skid it to the other side. It was hours of fun and the cause of a lot of bruises. Leg wrestling and trying to hit each other on the head with a spoon held between your teeth were other sports we enjoyed to pass the time.

It was also the first time any of us encountered weather on an epic and dangerous scale. On one occasion, Jennie and I were driving back from a Chicago shopping trip. The rain was biblical and the screen wipers couldn't cope. The gulleys on each side of the road were rivers. It seemed to come out of nowhere and we had never seen rain like it, even though we lived near Wales.

Lightning was ripping the sky apart and I saw my first fork lightning up close and personal as it hit the ground ahead of us. The radio stations were telling people to stay indoors and get under stairs or tables for safety. We were experiencing the start of a tornado.

Jennie and I made it to the nearest of the big houses and took cover. We called Ronnie and told him and the other guys to stay put in the studio and the other house. It blew over in about six hours and thankfully did not escalate to be one of the big ones. Still, it was pretty scary.

Recording Bridge Of Spies was a special experience for us all. We had over time gone into larger and larger studios as we worked with different people, but now we were recording on a grand scale. We put the drum kit in the convention centre next door in the hotel and ran the tie lines into the control room. We put mics on very tall stands in all the corners; that way we could record the ambience of the large room as well as the kit itself. The kit had 150 mics on it as well. RTB did not do things by halves. Tim was on a video link and headphones. It was quite isolating for him and always a long walk back to the control room. The drums on Bridge Of Spies are massive.

For the most part we had a ton of fun. There were a few blips however. Michael met a woman in a bar, a divorcee who had a clutch of kids and overnight he more or less moved in with her. From then on we had a bit of a job getting him into the studio on time, he was more interested in getting laid and fixing her car. It was all very sudden, very intense and very odd. It was like they were his kids. He barely knew them but now had a pop-up family. She was not your usual groupie, i.e. young and hot. She was middle-aged, had a complicated personal life and, well, was not hot at all. We were all very confused by the deep attachment he suddenly had. It was like the Moonies had their hooks in him.

Paul Jackson was a sensitive soul and quite shy. Paul got upset when Roy decided to put the bass riff for Heart & Soul back on to sequencers, as per the original demo. When we played live, Paul played the riff on bass very well, but he took it as a comment on his playing that the part got taken off him and put back onto machines, even though the song originally had that robotic sequence. It was the core of Heart & Soul. That episode took a bit of smoothing over.

Taj and I started to clash a bit as he was very strong-minded and so was I. He is also a very creative guitarist but I had firm ideas about how I wanted things played. Taj of course found that stifling. We were both full of good ideas but neither of us, then, had the maturity to work it out. We both just wanted our own way. I was definitely keeping a tight grip on everything as I was desperate for it all to be just right. I must have been a bloody nightmare to work with. I like to think that I have learned a lot about bringing out the best in my musicians since then.

Tim was a stoic star as ever. He was by his own admission not the most flamboyant of drummers but he was powerful, solid and got the job done. He was always keen to learn something new and always at pains to solve a problem, not add to it with any drama.

Ronnie was having a ball learning from Roy, who was always open-minded to his production ideas. Roy also had a great sense of humour and they did a lot of laughing.

I have often joked that Roy produced the album from behind a rack of lamb. Roy was a bon viveur and loved his food and drink. Almost every night he would have a rack of lamb with the little paper hats on the ends of the ribs and a good bottle of red wine. I swear to God if there had been a dog in the studio he would have chucked the bones to the dog over his shoulder à la Henry VIII. He would make his point on guitar riffs, keyboard parts and vocal harmonies by gesticulating with a rib in your direction. Roy loved to make up his own terminology for things. Just like the terms Wonderful Technicolour or Panavision, Roy decided that Bridge Of Spies was so amazing it had been recorded in 'Fabarama.' We liked that and our first tour was called 'The Fabarama Tour'.

Roy also introduced us to our first proper groupies, two Indian/

Top - Happy Days: Carol and brother Gary

Right - A babe in arms in Liverpool

Below - My Dad , Auntie Marie and my cousin Sean

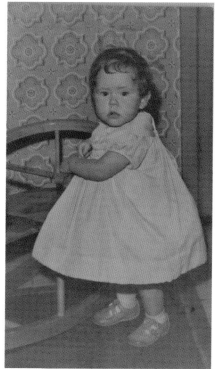

Top - Early years in Shropshire, with fiancé Tony and brother Gary

Right - Mum and Dad's wedding day

Below - Check the hair. Student days

Top - T'Pau and, erm, a helluva lot of booze. What happens on the road stays on the road.

Left - Taking America by storm with Heart and Soul

Bottom left - Hats off with Simon Hicks our A & R man

Bottom right - The price of looking beautiful

Above, left - An early promo shot of Ron and I. Above, right - NME cover.
The credible rock press initially loved us.

Bottom - How it all began. Working the clubs in between the bingo.

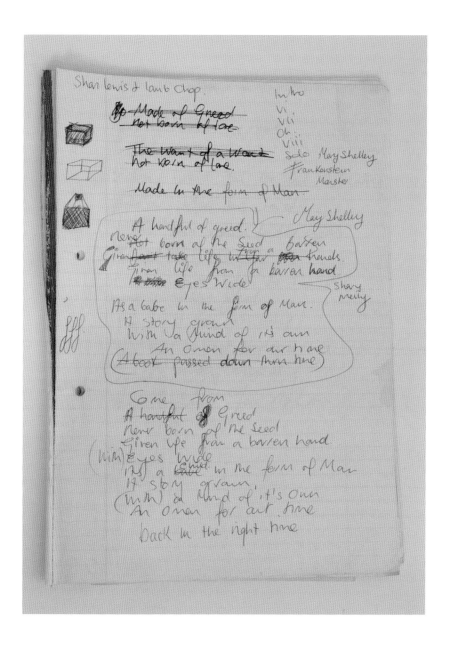

Who'd have thought that the words on this piece of paper would become my signature. An early draft of China.

Bling bling. Platinum discs, high heels and Champagne. On the rock'n'roll rollercoaster.

Top - The exceptionally talented Roy Thomas Baker

Bottom - Our first single reviews. Perfect.

Right, top to bottom - Access all areas. We were on the road for three or four years.

Top - Private planes became the norm - and they were usually well-stocked with Champagne

Left - The music magazine covers poured in

Above - Tower Records had life-sized icons of the band walking out of the window to launch Rage

Below - Rock stardom? Piece of cake.

Above - Rock'n'roll. Lippy on, hair looking gorgeous - another day at T'Pau
Central with Jennie and Tim.

Above left - We're talking big, we're Talking America

Above right - Sex talk? Possibly . . .

Above - Making the headlines around the world

Below - Helping Dad out with a football promotion with Tottenham and England star Gary Mabbutt

Bona fide rock
gods with
Chuck and
Di. Don't say
'cheese'. Say
'bitch'

Top - The record that became our theme tune, China In Your Hand, was written above a boathouse in Shrewsbury, with lyrics (opposite), penned on an A4 pad from the local stationer's

Left - Pain and pleasure in chiffon and leather

Frankenstein　　　　　　(China in your hand)

~~It~~ Was a dream he had.

has a ~~dream~~ ~~The~~ she had
about a scene he had
~~for immortal where it~~
that took ~~Please~~ ~~felt~~ in a foreign land
place
To take life on earth
to the second birth
And ~~no~~ man was in command.
A flight on the wings
of a young girls dreams
(the cradle of a vivid mind).
~~don't ~~hold~~ too hard~~
~~On the china in Your hand~~

That flew too far away.

fragile

If ~~Her~~ dream comes true
　　　　　Your dream
(but ~~Tonight~~ comes true one day)

If Her dream comes true

We Could ~~make the~~ Monster live again
We May push to hard

Above - RTB was at the controls, but soon we took control of our own sound

Left - We were the favourite band of the nation's pop press

American sisters from Chicago who were great fun, really cool, pretty, and charming company. They were courtesans essentially.

They took me and Jennie shopping in Chicago, showing us the hippest shops and the coolest eateries and bars. Roy would often send a car for them and bring them over to the studio. We'd all hit the bars in Wisconsin or Lake Geneva. I really enjoyed their company, but also knew that they would happily sleep with my man without batting an eye. I did not let that opportunity arise. As for the rest of the boys, well, I wouldn't know.

The hotel was a regular stop-off point for most of the big bands who were touring the States. It was a reasonably luxurious hotel, if a tad 'golfy'. I remember one night, we were all in the hotel bar and at that time you could smoke in bars. Ronnie smoked roll-ups. I had quit by then to save my voice. We were at the bar, Ronnie was making a roll-up, when in walked a large group of rock'n'rollers. They looked like a band, but I didn't know who they were; everybody had a leather jacket and a perm back then. A guy in a flat cap with really curly hair, that turned out not to be a perm, stood beside us at the bar and asked Ronnie in a Geordie accent if his tobacco was Golden Virginia. It was Brian Johnson and the band with him was AC/DC.

They'd been on tour for many months and Brian had long since run out of English cigarettes. He asked Ronnie for a roll-up. Angus Young jokingly asked him if he'd done time as the roll-up was so very thin. Ronnie has really long, elegant fingers and he could roll the most perfect, skinny cigarettes. Cons in prison used to have to make their 'baccy' last so they'd have to make really skinny roll-ups.

We ended up spending the whole night with AC/DC, bonded by rolling tobacco.

We were living our dreams. There we were, recording our first album and hanging out with giants of the business. But they were totally unstarry and the evening was very natural, just like a lively night in a bar with mates. AC/DC are not the tallest guys in the world but that did not stop them from having the tallest, most model-like groupies. Eventually, the evening came to an end at around 2am and we all said goodbye. As we watched the band stagger off with their groupies towering over them, they looked more like female security guards than women that they were about to sleep with. I thought: 'My God, girls will f- anybody if they're in a rock'n'roll band, even if they only come up to their navel.'

The album was progressing well with most of us enjoying the process. Simon Hicks, our A and R guy, flew out for a few days to take a listen. We had to play him the work-so-far. Those occasions were always tricky as it felt like an intrusion into our creative process. Besides, we really didn't give a toss about the label's opinion. 'You have recognised that we have talent now kindly leave us to it!' It was our mission to get Simon drunk. He was very straight-laced. He had done a degree in theology and how he ended up in the music 'biz I don't know. We did manage to get a few margaritas down him one night and talked him into a game of Skid-rug!

We did have one problem though, we had a song that just was not working out. We just could not get it to live up to the potential we all thought it had. The industry terminology for that is 'polishing a turd.' It doesn't matter how long you polish it for, it's still a turd.

So we were a song short. Roy asked Ronnie and I if we had any more songs he had not heard. I had a cassette in my bag of a piano vocal idea that we had started before we left the UK. It was a very simple vocal, no harmonies, and Ronnie had roughed out the chords on the piano. It was China In Your Hand. Roy instantly thought it was a fantastic song. I had most of the lyrics for it, it just needed a little tidying up. Ronnie had to teach Michael the piano part, which he embellished. The other guys learned the chords and we started to get it down. It grew and grew by the day. We added pizzicato strings on the front, keyboard choir voices, layers and layers of guitar harmonies, our massive drum sound in the chorus and a big old break. Sax was big in the '80s. It was considered grown-up and classy. I liked it, it saved the day and helped us to complete our album. I was happy with all of the songs, but for me it was always Heart & Soul that I couldn't wait for people to hear.

After three months in Lake Geneva, the album was finally finished. I did not want that time to end. We had got used to living there, our routine and the little world we had created. Michael had to leave his new family!

The band headed home with Jennie to the UK. Roy invited Ronnie and I to New York to see our first album being mastered.

OK here's the science bit. Mastering is a post-production process where you finalise the volume levels of the songs relative to each other, and then the volume of the whole album is set, equalised and compressed. So basically you don't have either anything sonically jumping out at you or, equally, disappearing. It is from that mastered audio file that all copies are taken. It is a dark art and there are some mastering legends. George Marino mastered Bridge Of Spies at Sterling Sound, NYC. He's mastered for John Lennon, AC/DC, Whitney Houston, Bon Jovi , Motley Crew, Coldplay, Metallica, Guns 'n' Roses, Journey . . . the list goes on and on. He was The Man. I am very proud to be on the auspicious list of artists whose work he made sound the very best it could. George very sadly died in 2012.

After the mastering was done, Roy invited Ronnie and I to stay with him and his wife Terri in LA. He had a fabulous house on Sunset Plaza Drive. I'd never been to a house with a pool. I didn't know anyone that well off. I'd seen them in hotels, of course, but never at a house. Roy's garden had a Japanese design. The jacuzzi was built high up among rocks and you could jump out of that into the pool. And he had a proper bar in his house, not just a bottle of wine.

Ronnie and I had our own guest cottage known as The Freddie Mercury Suite, as Freddie often stayed there. The house was open-plan, everything including the carpets, was white. In the living room there was a clear Perspex grand piano that you could either play or it played itself. It was the sort of house I had only ever seen on TV. I had no idea some people actually lived like this. It was bliss.

Ronnie and I were staying for a week. Roy had a few business things to attend to. One morning he asked Ronnie if he had a clean driving licence. Ron said he did, so Roy threw him the keys to his Rolls Royce and said: 'Pick me up at the Staples Center at 2pm, try not to crash it.' We had our own Freddie Mercury cottage and now a Rolls Royce to drive. Had we died and gone to heaven? What we didn't realise was that the band felt very left out, not being invited. It was the subtle start of an ever-widening gap.

On our last night Roy took us to Spago, THE celeb restaurant of the day. We were hanging out with Motley Crue. I was, as usual, trying to keep up with the men and they were all drinking Sambuca, which I'd never drunk before. I had about 10 of them. I ate all the coffee beans that float on the top and get set on fire as well. The next morning it was time to leave and catch a plane home. I was in a really bad way. Somehow I packed my case and climbed into the back of the Roller. I was a very nasty shade of green and just lay on the back seat groaning. Roy kept saying: 'Carol, please, please don't throw up in my Rolls Royce.' It all got too much for me so he pulled over and I threw open the car door and managed to hurl up on the road. I think I missed the Rolls, though I may have splashed the paintwork a bit.

Due to the routing of our airline tickets to the UK we had to fly back to Chicago from LA to get home. That involved catching an internal flight on the now defunct People Express Airline. If I say they make Ryanair seem upmarket, you'll get some idea of how hideous it was. They specialised in hiring the rudest cabin crew with the hugest backsides that would bump into your head if you were in an aisle seat. A request for peanuts would be greeted with them being thrown at you. It was similar to being at the checkout at an Aldi supermarket. I was, of course, in a very fragile state as we flew back to O'Hare. When the trolley dollies came through I asked for a glass of water. 'Sorry Ma'am what was that?' 'A glass of water please'. 'Sorry Ma'am I can't quite . . .' Ok, I thought, shorten your sentence: 'Water please.' She turned to Ronnie and said: 'I'm sorry sir I can't understand what she's saying?' I raised my voice and said 'H2O . . . in a GLASS!' . . . 'Oh whaddah, why didn't you say so in the first place?' ARRRRGGGHHH! We experienced being cousins divided by a common language many times in The States.

Once, when having a headache in New York and needing pills – and let me tell you, they do the BEST headache pills over there, I love Advil! – I asked on the street to be directed to a chemist and was asked if I needed a university professor. When we were on tour, we were in a bar one night and our normally-shy bass player Paul was holding court, surrounded by girls laughing. We edged closer to hear what on earth he was saying to make them all crack up. One girl said: 'Go on say car boot again.' Whereas we know that drugstore means chemist, and sidewalk means pavement, and car boot means trunk, things don't translate the other way around.

Ronnie and I caught our connecting flight back to the UK. We flew through a Transatlantic storm so violent our seat belts could not hold us in our seats. We had to hook our arms under the seat arms to stay sat down. We were buffeted so hard the crew could not get up from their seats to assist or comfort distressed passengers. The overhead lockers shunted open and luggage started to fall out. People were crying. Ronnie and I were deathly silent. I do remember trying to drink a vodka tonic, well if I was going to die I might as well numb the pain, but it kept leaping out of my glass. The storm went on for what seemed like an eternity but was most likely about an hour. When it was over the captain admitted over the speakers that, in all his flying career, that had been his most scary experience and he praised everyone for keeping calm. I ordered another vodka tonic.

We hadn't seen the last of America and found ourselves back in the States on The Fabarama tour not long after we'd recorded Bridge Of Spies.

Safely back home, we released Heart & Soul as our debut single in the UK. It bombed, slipping out of the lower reaches of the charts almost as quickly as it had entered. David Betteridge, the MD of Siren, loathed the sound of the record. Roy had put a lot of compression on it, which made it sound great on radio, particularly out in the States. But it had changed the sound. It didn't sound as rich as it did in the studio. I must admit when we got home, after all the excitement of recording and mastering it, I struggled to listen to it on our stereo. I had to keep fiddling with the treble and the bass to get it right. I couldn't understand why it sounded like an assault on my ears. David Betteridge heard it and he was livid. He said: 'f-in hell that's awful.' He was livid with Roy, whom he thought should have known better with all his experience. So when Heart

& Soul bombed, he felt very justified in his comments.

But if you hear it on the radio to this day, Roy's production on our records keeps them sounding current. But that was no help at the start of our recording career. Right then we thought it was all over before it had begun. We thought Siren were going to drop us.

In the States, however, the story was different. The US of A was falling in love with us. Heart & Soul was released directly on Virgin Records and started to climb the Billboard chart. Our American record company wanted us to go on a long promo tour and we were flown out for a major league press junket.

I wasn't surprised that America fell for Heart & Soul, it's a fantastic song, but I was devastated that the UK didn't. When I heard that for the first time after we'd recorded it and had it mixed, it blew my mind. I'd never heard anything like it. That was the moment when I knew we were going to get somewhere. I joke on stage now that not a lot of people know that I invented rap: me and Debbie Harry, with Rapture. It still sounds great on the radio even now. For me, that's our shining moment as songwriters. It really is. However my confidence was sorely tested after it dropped out of the UK chart even though I was vindicated in the States.

Virgin America were determined to make it work and it became a huge hit. Eventually, Heart & Soul also got to number four hear at home and reached the top five in most European territories too. The song got chosen by Pepe Jeans for their very cool cinema commercial campaign – I knew all those years of selling jeans would pay off eventually. So we got a second chance at home in the UK.

Success in America started to happen while we were back at home in Shrewsbury licking our wounds after the single had fallen out of the UK Top 100. We weren't really doing anything and didn't know what would happen next. Everybody was reeling from the disappointment.

Based on the buzz around Heart & Soul, a tour was quickly put together by our agent, the late Ian Copeland, brother to Miles and Stuart. We were flown out to LA for a heavy schedule of radio promotion. Then we went home again before going back to the States to do a three-month tour. We had the grottiest, smelliest tour bus in the world and we loved it. We were just playing in rock clubs, nightclubs and sports bars all over the country. It was really starting to take off as Heart & Soul climbed to number four on the Billboard chart. It stayed on the charts for months, going up and down and up and down. The thing about having a hit single in The States is that it's a massive continent. So you can be doing brilliantly in New York but at the same time not be doing so well say in Florida. In this country for example, Heart Radio has the same playlist all over the country. But over there, the stations could do what they liked. So our success really varied from state to state.

We were invited to radio parties with the likes of Debbie Harry and started to enjoy living the high life. We flew out to LA on Virgin First Class. At that time, Richard Branson owned Virgin Airlines and Virgin Records, so any Virgin artist flew First Class. It was absolutely amazing. I had become used to holidays abroad as a kid. But we were the Freddy Laker package tour family. We were always on charter flights to the big resorts in Spain or Italy. At the time, I considered that to be very exciting, as I was too small then to worry about legroom. But now we were flying First Class and I could not get over it. I was like the cat with the cream.

There were on-board therapists going round the cabin giving us neck massages. I'm sure the boys hoped they were going to get a blow job as well. The First Class cabin was like a proper restaurant with a bar. We weren't just sitting there with our little plastic trays in front of us. It was seriously posh. There was a bar in the middle of the deck and we propped it up for the entire 11-hour flight and they didn't stop serving us. We were shit-faced by the time we got to the other side. We didn't get out of order, we were just really, really giggly. We tried very hard to hide that from the stern, po-faced immigration officers when we made it through passport control.

We thought back to earlier years and to our time with Kingsley, at Rockfield. Just like he'd predicted, we were now, in fact, Talking America. Our dream was coming true.

Appearing on MTV was a really big deal. It was only two years old and was the new music platform, where you could see as well as hear artists. MTV threw a huge party down on the beach near Santa Monica.

They had the cameras there and there was a bar, and they'd set up a stage. Mick Jones, ex of the Sex Pistols was there with his band and they were trying to play a song but were shockingly bad. Their drummer couldn't play in time at all, so they kept stopping after about 16 bars and starting it over and over again. It was really funny. I think they may have been a bit tiddly.

We had to play cricket on the beach because we were English. It was really corny. Sand was going everywhere. But I just loved the energy of America and now I was getting to visit all the places I'd seen on the telly. I loved the glamour. I loved the bigger and better. I loved their social culture, like Happy Hour where you could prop up a bar and have chicken wings and dips and chips and drinks. You have to remember that all this was not common back home then, so it seemed really exotic to me. I loved that whole environment. It was fun!

The record company was taking us everywhere and wining and dining us. We were being taken to the best places to eat and drink. We'd gone from being on the dole, eating fish finger sarnies and having no heating in our flat to flying to the States First Class and being picked up in a limo.

When we were in Texas on our way to an in-store record signing, our limo broke down in the middle of the road. We were baking hot and almost had steam coming out of our ears. The driver called for a cab and somehow we got to the record store. It was just like the famous scene from the film Spinal Tap. We turned up to do our signing and there was nobody there. There were crash barriers to hold back a crowd that didn't exist. There was a table with a beautiful white cloth on it. There were six stations of albums, photographs, Champagne and Sharpies. And by that time, we were riding high in the charts. But not one person came.

Eventually, we saw the manager whispering in the ears of the staff, telling them to get things signed. The staff were coming up and asking us to sign one for their son, one for a cousin etc, etc. It was so embarrassing. Despite our Billboard position, the support was still patchy. The local record company rep became like Tap's Arnie Phuffkin character saying: 'Kick my ass, this is my fault, go on give it a good kick'. What made it even worse was that the record store owner then said he had even flown a biplane around the area trailing a big 'Meet T'Pau' banner and STILL nobody gave a shit.

We also had a 'Hello Cleveland!' moment. The backstage area of a theatre gig we were playing had copious rooms and corridors. We got called to the stage and it took us 10 minutes to find it, we even went past the same janitor twice. If you haven't seen Spinal Tap you have to watch the movie. I can tell you that all those embarrassing mishaps have happened to all bands.

At the other end of the scale: Tower Records LA had my face large as you like in the window. I felt like Madonna. LA was brilliant fun to hang out in. Once again we went to Roy's house but this time the whole band and crew came too. However our show at the prestigious Roxy club was a disaster. The Roxy is LA's version of London's long-gone but much-lamented Marquee Club. Small, hot, sweaty and with the stickiest floor, it was an essential step on the road to success. There was all this hype around us by now: The Brits are coming! The late great Casey Kasem was playing us constantly on his America's Hot 40 TV show. The video was on heavy rotation. We were permanently on MTV. It was all looking good and that show should have cemented our reputation as an up-and-coming band that justified the hype.

Chris Cooke was looking after a few acts by now and one of the other people he was managing was the saxophonist from the Average White Band, Molly Duncan. Chris suggested to us that when we played the Roxy, Molly should play the sax break on China, as well as some of the other brass parts on other songs. We couldn't afford to take a sax player on the road so just did without and had a guitar lead break on China. We thought having a sax was a great idea, especially as the Average White Band had been massive in the States. The kudos would be terrific.

I asked: 'When can Molly come and rehearse, when can we get together?' Chris said: 'Oh, don't worry about him rehearsing, he's really busy, he'll just learn it, it will all be fine.' There were shades of the Scotty incident again and it made me nervous. I like to prepare for things in advance but he was Molly Duncan, experienced muso' from a revered band, so we decided to just be relaxed about it. We thought we had nothing to fear. You know, Average White Band, Pick Up The Pieces, what could go wrong? But it was worrying that he didn't even turn up for our sound check. That was really sailing close to the wind. We began our set and the monitors were awful, none of us could hear each other or ourselves. I was over-singing to get above the band and it wasn't a 'vibey' show. We were all on edge and the crowd were not impressed. The reception was tepid.

So we came to the sax break in China In Your Hand. The song had a false end before the lead break began. I announced: 'Please welcome on stage from Average White Band, Molly Duncan!' Tim brought the song back in with a big drum roll. Cue Molly. Oh God, no: he was off his tits. It sounded like he was blowing through a comb and paper. I just stood looking at the floor. Ronnie, of course, was pissing himself laughing. But I was furious. He absolutely screwed our show. I wanted him off the stage but he was parping away, ruining the other songs too.

We got the most awful reviews for the Roxy and it killed us in LA. You get one chance and that was ours. It's like playing London and New York. The critics are always at those shows ready to pounce.

The rest of that tour was the best fun with many highlights. We supported Thompson Twins at a big outdoor show in Texas. In Cleveland we played October Fest with Cutting Crew who had just been at number one in the States with '(I just) Died In Your Arms Tonight'. They were the hot band of the moment. The stage was on a riverbank and the audience were on the opposing bank or floating past us in boats. We had a backstage artist enclosure and a really young female Cutting Crew fan was waving frantically from the other side the fence. She begged Ronnie to get a backstage picture of Cutting Crew. She told him she had one frame left on her film in the camera. Ronnie took her camera and walked off into the dressing room area. He then got the rest of T'Pau to drop their pants and bend over, mooning the camera and took the last shot on the film. Taking the camera back to the girl, now in tears of gratitude he said 'Nick (Van Ede) sends his love'.

Twigletgate

On our first American press junket there was all sorts of Trekkie weirdness. A lot of people picked up on the name and made the connection between T'Pau and Star Trek. They were way ahead of us with all those Trekkie conventions and comicon-style events. So wherever I went they thought I must be a Trekkie, a Star Trek super fan. They assumed I knew all the different episodes and all the different dates. And I actually knew nothing.

We were in New York staying at the Warwick hotel on Seventh Avenue. I had been allocated a room for all my interviews. This guy came in with his briefcase, he was a very quiet, timid sort of journalist. He sat down opposite me. He placed his briefcase between us and lifted up the lid, I couldn't see what was inside. I just assumed he was looking for his notebook or pens or something like that. Then all of a sudden he just reached in and pulled out two plastic pointy Vulcan ears and put them on. Then he got his notebook out, closed the lid down and started asking questions about the band and the album. But he made no reference to his ears. There was no: 'Hey, look at me, I'm a crazy Trekkie just like you!' So I looked at him and he looked at me and we had a perfectly normal conversation about the band and the making of the record. Then at the end of the interview he said: 'Thank you Miss Decker for your time. I love the album. Good luck.' He opened his briefcase, silently put his ears back in, then closed the briefcase, shook my hand and left. Neither of us made any reference to his Vulcan ears.

Virgin Records latched on to the Star Trek connection as they thought it was a good marketing tool. Heart & Soul, the single in America, had the 'live long and prosper' Vulcan hand sign on the cover. I used to fight against it because I didn't want people to think I was an f-ing nerd.

But now I've got children myself and my daughter's been to one of those sci-fi events and she's totally into it. It's almost like an alternative universe and I've realised that the people who are into all that are very passionate and very sweet. So what if they want to bury their heads in their own made-up world, these days I wouldn't blame them. They don't do anybody any harm. But back then, I wanted to be taken seriously as an artist. Instead I was just dogged with all this Trekkie shit.

Being on the road for so long taught us a few lessons about what it's like to be in a successful band. Until then, we'd always been on the fringes. We'd seen people like Robert Plant and the South Wales Massive, but we'd never had a hit ourselves. So for the first time, we found out how we would react to being successful. When there was a huge painting of me in the window of Tower Records, in LA, I was actually startled to see it. I caught my breath. If you see your face on a billboard, it's quite something. A bit later on in our career, it happened again when Tower Records, in London's Piccadilly, filled the window with giant images of us to launch our second platinum album, Rage.

It was a massive poster of the album cover with the six of us striding towards the public, looking like we were coming through the window.

I started to feel my own might. I don't know if that's arrogance. You know, but I would walk into a room and people would turn their heads and whisper. It's intoxicating when it happens. You've got to keep a light touch, otherwise you can get a bit too big for your own boots and I'm perfectly happy to accept that I probably did from time to time. There were times when my inner bossy knickers went wild. You know, the prefect and the lifeguard were now famous and influential too.

Your ego grows exponentially. I could go on a charm offensive and be absolutely delightful company. I could also be a brat, because that impatient side of my personality was getting fed too. I was very quickly getting accustomed to people pretty much letting me get what I wanted, particularly in the States where they were all over me like a cheap suit. They really love fame.

On one occasion, we were in a restaurant on tour when a bunch of young girls recognised us and wanted autographs. Afterwards I went to the loo and a middle-aged woman followed me in and asked: 'Excuse me, are you somebody?' She wanted my autograph but had no idea who I was.

Today it would be the dreaded selfie and yes I have been approached in the 'Lav for one of those too.

Touring is really intense. I am not offering that up as an excuse for bad behaviour but you do get really fatigued on a very deep level. You are working hard and shows are emotionally and physically draining. The time between soundcheck and show time is a no man's land. You don't quite know what to do with yourself. I can never relax as I just want to get on with it. I used to have a glass of wine or two with dinner, but I never really did the serious Dutch Courage drinking and drugging before a show as I wouldn't have been able to sing well if I did. I get anxious before a show and all I do is focus on what I have to do.

I don't like to see guests beforehand either. I am not in the right headspace to chat. Afterwards, of course, we partied hard. Being on tour also means living and working with the same people 24/7, so now and again tempers could fray. When you are burned out you can see your arse quite quickly over the smallest of things. If some nonchalant waiter pisses you off or if they don't have the drink you wanted or if something doesn't come fast enough, you mouth off. I certainly could be a bit short at times. You do have to learn to get a bit of a grip on yourself. There were other things that bring you back down to earth, you know, like the Texas limo breaking down and then the in-store signing where nobody turned up. That brought us back down. But apart from those little things, everything else was starting to click. We knew that our singles would do well and that people would take us to the best places and give us what we wanted. Everything was becoming a given.

I had another Spinal Tap moment on tour in Europe. You know, the scene where the meat is too big for guitarist Nigel Turner's bread? That happened to me.

I always had Twiglets as part of my rider in my dressing room. When we started doing bigger tours, we took our own tour catering with us so we didn't have to make do with what the venues would provide for us. The caterers would stock up on all our favourite snacks so we had a little bit of home on the road. My little treat to myself was Twiglets because I love crunchy things and I love Marmite; hey presto! That's Twiglets!

So there would always be a bowl of Twiglets in my dressing room. We were on tour in Germany somewhere, I can't remember where, one town was blending into another. One night I had a bowl of . . . crisps! And I absolutely saw my arse. 'Why have I got crisps? Where are my Twiglets? Who's in charge around here? What's going on? If I'd wanted crisps I'd have asked for fucking crisps. I asked for Twiglets. And these are fucking cheese and onion crisps, which I fucking hate! Where are my fucking Twiglets?'

Jennie my best friend and tour manager looked at me squarely and said: 'Oh really, and is your meat too big for your bread, Carol?' We both burst out laughing and I just realised that I was being a bit bad tempered. I had to learn that those things didn't really matter.

But you do get a bit all-powerful. You get used to things going your way. And when things don't go your way, all of a sudden you're in a position to be unpleasant to somebody about it, and a couple of times I probably was a bit of a twat.

Out in the States some of the radio stations are massive. They have a huge listenership and are very influential. Back then, there were 5,000 radio stations in America and one station on our itinerary was based in Atlanta. A big station was throwing a 'meet and greet' and we just had to turn up, have photos taken and say 'hi' to fans. Cyndi Lauper was there, so was Taylor Dane and so were several other artists of note. We were all being brought onto this stage at the same time to say 'hi' to the fans and the crowd before we mingled. Leaning up against the wall, quietly watching, was Debbie Harry. I was having my hair 'froofed' by a stylist when I noticed her. I said 'hello' to the coolest woman in the world. She said: 'Hey, how are you, great tune by the way.' It blew my mind. Debbie Harry knew who I was. Ok, well, possibly not, but she knew Heart & Soul. And she liked it.

We were in America for three months on a pretty low budget tour. We had a really dodgy old tour bus but it felt like home.

A tour bus is a moving party. We'd finish a show, load up the gear and start drinking though the night on the way to the next town. Every three to four days we would get a hotel room for a night, to shower and get some proper sleep. We were in so many Holiday Inns and they all had the same layout. Several of us tried to get into last night's room in the previous town with that night's key in a different town. We would frequently be on the same bill as The Truth. They were signed to IRS records, Miles Copeland's label, and Ian Copeland, Miles' brother, was also their US agent as well as ours. We made a nice little package. Their tour bus was as rundown as ours and definitely smellier. They were great lads and we had a few beers on those nights, I can tell you. We became regular card players. I like Gin Rummy and the boys played poker. One night Ronnie and I had gone to bed and we heard raised voices in the back lounge of the bus. Dean and Paul were having a blazing row. Paul had started to get a bit bored and not play properly. They had been playing for money and Dean was in for £500. Gambling was then banned. It was matchsticks after that night.

The journeys could be exceptionally long. Once travelling through Texas, a range of mountains in the distance never seemed to get any closer leading Ronnie to comment that they were painted on the windscreen. Sometimes we would go to bed in one state – as opposed to a total state – and wake up in another, hundreds of miles from where we started out. I naïvely asked Jennie how our driver stayed awake all night. She replied: 'How do you think?'

The morning we drove over Brooklyn Bridge into Manhattan I sat beside our driver. It was 5am and the sky was cloudless and blue. The ferocious early morning sun bounced off the skyscrapers, making them look like mirrors on fire. New York is a rock star. I had always dreamed of coming here. I fell in love with its noise, smells, height, craziness and abruptness. The first time I went in an elevator that sped to the top of the MTV building I felt queasy, like my stomach had gone down as I went up. At the Carnegie Deli, I got yelled at for not ordering my sandwich fast enough. Someone had their bag snatched just behind us as we walked down 7th Ave. We played cricket in Central Park one afternoon. When we got back to our tour hotel, we saw on the news that someone had been murdered right in the same place a few hours later. The avenues had huge potholes in them, covered by random sheets of metal to stop cars and people falling in them. Steam poured out of vents in the pavement just like in the movies. I felt like I was in a film. The noise level was loud and constant. It was a crazy town at that time. New York was dangerous and bankrupt. I loved it.

Heart & Soul was our ticket to the top and life couldn't have been sweeter. Ronnie and me were fine; we were living our dream together. We had a great time out there. The other guys were all married so it was difficult for them. Dean had two babies, so that was tough. At one point the wives flew out to join us and it was hell on earth. They didn't fit in and they didn't understand. We took a few days off so the band could be with their wives and get some nuptials. Several of the wives just didn't understand the pressure that we were under, and I think they resented the dedication we all had to the band. They didn't like the fact that their husbands spent more time working than they did with them. I am sure, looking back, that they felt they were in second place to the family we had become. Years later I got to talk that through with a couple of them and we made our peace and they were terribly apologetic. But back then I had more knives in my back than Julius Caesar. It all seemed to be my fault. I wasn't providing a great opportunity for us all, as far as they were concerned, I was just full of myself. I was in a successful band, I was getting to be famous and a couple of them were simply jealous cats. The others just kept quiet. I did not feel welcome in their company, which I deeply resented on my own tour.

Then something happened. We were in the Mid West and by now Heart & Soul had been re-released in the UK and was climbing the UK charts. Top Of The Pops wanted us on the show. We had few days off and were told to pack a few things because we were flying home to do the show and a couple of interviews. We were told we'd then fly straight back to carry on the US tour. We did our first TOTP, which was a huge moment for all of us. We had all grown up watching it, and those of a certain age will remember that TOTP was the only major UK music show at the time. It was a career maker. We were deliriously happy that our home country was finally coming to appreciate us.

We were taken out for a big celebratory meal by Chris and Siren.

After supper, and a goodly amount of backslapping and drinking, we asked what time our flight was back to America. Chris Cooke said: 'You're not going back.' We were dumbstruck. 'What?' We had left all our clothes out there, the boys' wives were still out there, and Jennie and the crew were waiting to carry on the tour. Tim didn't even have his house keys and his wife was on the tour bus. We were told we were not going back because things were going really well at home and the record was starting to really pick up in Europe too. We were told it would be better if we stayed at home and spread across the UK and Europe. But you don't do that to the Americans. Your reputation is very quickly rubbished if you let them down. You do not fuck with American promoters. They had to cancel shows and issue refunds on tickets, not something a promoter or band ever wants to do. And for no good reason. No one was ill, I had not lost my voice and there had been no tragic accident. We just didn't go back because we didn't want to is how it appeared to them.

Our name was mud because we never went back and finished our tour. It was a big mistake. It made no sense to us, if you make it big in the States then you usually make it big across the rest of the world anyway. And it was utter folly. We started to become uncomfortable with some of the decisions that were being made for us and also the sense of power that some of the people around us seemed to have. We suddenly felt we were being treated like children. We had been told to get on a plane to the UK, do this very important show then we'd fly straight back to the States. But there had been no intention of sending us back.

Our tour manager, Jennie, had to pack all our stuff, ship all our equipment home and explain everything to the bitchy wives, who got told their husbands had gone back to England and wouldn't be coming back. It was a nightmare.

Despite all of that, our first TOTP was an amazing experience. It was a first for all of us to appear on that institution-of-a-programme that so many generations of music lovers had watched. BBC TV was then at the White City building, near Shepherd's Bush. The White City building was practically a circle and I used to get terribly lost in it. There were lots of different levels and about every 200 yards there'd be a coffee point, almost like a canteen, for all the different studios. It was surprisingly dull and quiet and not very rock and roll at all. All the people in the building were either engineers or back office people. I thought when I walked through the doors for the first time that everybody would be having a party. I thought it would be teeming with cool actors and hip pop stars. But it wasn't. And it was much dominated by the unions. We used to have to sneak our make-up artist in as my personal assistant because we had to use the union staff for everything. The make-up artists were very old fashioned then and would make everybody look like Marie Osmond with blue eye shadow, pink cheeks and Tammy Wynette hair, all backcombed and lacquered. You couldn't touch your own musical equipment either. I remember Tim sitting on the stage and just trying to get the kit right for himself. He moved the cymbals and adjusted the snare and started to pull it closer but the union guy was all over him like a rash: 'I'll do that, don't touch the kit.' You couldn't pick your own bottle of water up and move it around, you had to ask somebody else to do it for you. And we had to rehearse over and over all day. You had to run through your section of the show, then the other artists would rehearse their section of the show and then we'd all rehearse the entire show. It went out live on a Thursday so they had to have it just right. So we'd be there all day and be shattered by the time the show was ready to go on air. It was absolutely knackering.

A few of the bigger artists and some of the American artists seemed to be excused the treadmill of run-throughs. The Bee Gees, for instance, didn't have to do any at all. When we were on the show with them we were not even allowed in the studio when they recorded their bit. We were gently but firmly pushed aside as their massive burly bodyguards with huge Ceelo Green white smiles put their hands in the small of our backs and said: 'Hey how ya' doin'? Bee Gees comin' through now; thank you, yes, lookin' good, step aside, Bee Gees comin' through.' I have never been so nicely shoved out of the way. It was so exciting, I couldn't believe I was in the famous studio that as a child I'd seen so many programmes being made in. There were huge gigantic cameras that glided on massive big grey podiums. They were like Daleks skidding around the room. And then there were the famous Radio One DJs: Bruno

Brookes and Steve Wright, and Simon Bates, Mike Smith and Mike Read. Thank the Lord Jimmy Saville was long gone. That man always gave me the creeps even as a young child watching him on the TV.

One of my most treasured memories of a TOTP TV appearance was the Christmas edition. The show was made up of a collection of artists with the biggest hits of that year and we'd been the highest-ranking number one of 1987. They got us a beautiful white baby grand piano for Michael. I had some tinsel round my neck. We had smuggled Champagne into our dressing room and we were very, very happy that day.

Bigger Than The Beatles

We went on to perform on TOTP many times over the years. Once when we were rehearsing China In Your Hand, Paul and Linda McCartney were in the studio. They did not take their eyes off me for over an hour. I thought: 'Yeah I got it going on, even The Beatles are impressed.' When we finished rehearsing it was time for a break. Paul and Linda came over to me and said that they were sorry if they were freaking me out but I reminded them so much of their little girl, Stella. I never thought she and I looked alike at all. We both just have red hair, but hey if it made them feel better to hang out with me then fine! We went to one of the funny little canteens, Linda and I got a table and Paul queued up to get us all disgusting BBC coffee in Styrofoam cups.

After that, whenever Paul and I were at a showbiz bash, he would always come over and say 'hi'. I couldn't believe it. I never wanted to bother him so I would wave from afar. He knows the impact he has on people and always went out of his way to put you at ease. Linda used to send me a Christmas calendar of her photographs and drop me a line now and again. Over time we lost touch, as you do with showbiz friends, but it was nice for a while being pals with Macca.

Heart & Soul was the single that helped us to break through internationally. It went top five in most of Europe. The boys in the band occasionally got a few days off but I never stopped. Sometimes I had to do things on my own. I flew out to Italy with Clark Datchler from Johnny Hates Jazz. They were having a hit with Shattered Dreams. Clarke and I were on our own doing promotional interviews at radio stations across Italy. We were staying at a beautiful hotel in Milan. He arranged for a red rose to be put on my pillow. We had been getting on very well, I think he was hoping to get on even better.

A huge boost to the success of Heart & Soul and the band's profile was being picked to be the opening act for Nik Kershaw on his Radio Musicola tour. Nik had had huge success by then with Human Racing and The Riddle. We were – and are – huge fans. He is an incredibly-talented songwriter and musician. We were quite intimidated by his success and I bought a whole new outfit just for the tour, complete with cowboy boots with spurs and chains on. I thought I looked the dog's bollocks but they did 'chink' a lot when I walked.

At the venue there was a long corridor to catering. I was chinking along it and as I entered, the dining room fell silent. Nik smiled and said: 'New boots Carol?' Everyone burst out laughing and I felt a bit of a knob.

The first show we did was at The Forum, or Town and Country Club as it was called then. I was so nervous that all the spit left my mouth and my top lip stuck to my top teeth. After the show, I went to meet my family and my Mum asked me why I kept smiling all through the set.

It was our first big support tour and his crew played many jokes on us, in keeping with the touring tradition of 'treat the support like shit'.

The worst thing they did to us was to put a fish on top of our van engine. It was a bleak winter in early 1987. There was lots of snow and it was bloody freezing so naturally we cranked the heater up when we hit the road.

We had just played the Hammersmith Odeon, the final gig of the tour.

It was really cold and icy out by the load out door. A couple of Nik's normally unhelpful crew were surprisingly helpful that night with our load out. Later we pushed off to our hotel. Dear God the smell when the heater got going. Bastards. The fish was cooked to a crisp.

When we were headlining our own tours a year later, we hired almost every one of that crew. They were evil but excellent. But we also played an end of tour joke. Nik had a very serious ecological song called Save The Whale. Ronnie had bought a kids bathtub whale and attached it a remote control car. As the lights went down and Nik started this very sombre tribute to the great leviathan, Ronnie's plastic whale went squeaking across the front of the stage. Nik booted it into the audience. He did not laugh that night, though I have made him laugh a lot since!

Although Heart & Soul was a huge breakthrough song for us, China In Your Hand was the one that changed the game. It changed all of our lives. Its chart positions were 43 – 19 – 5 – 1. That, as they say in the 'biz, is a song with legs. We had started to promote China in the UK. We knew it was also doing well in Europe but sadly not in America. They didn't get it. The radio pluggers were complaining that nobody knew what we were. Are you a rap band? Are you a rock band? They had to format you on American radio. They are confused by eclecticism. Our moment in the American sun was over.

Siren wanted to get us on a big European support tour and they managed to buy us on to Bryan Adams' Into The Fire tour. If we were intimidated by Nik's set up, that went up another league. Bryan only played arenas; 12,000 to 15,000-seaters. It was utterly terrifying. His crew and tour manager barely had any time for us. They were paid to make sure that Bryan's show went as smoothly as it should and we were not their responsibility. The support had to cause as little bother as possible, get on, play and then fuck off. The headline act, on the other hand, had all their gear set up onstage from soundcheck. The support could not move anything and had to play in whatever space was left on the stage. We also only ever had about 15 minutes to soundcheck. By the time Bryan's band were done soundchecking, the doors to the venue would be opening 15 to 20 minutes later. That's all the time we had to get our gear on to the stage, plug it in, make sure it was working and quickly bash out a chorus to something. It was pretty brutal.

When we played our first Wembley Arena with him, our meagre sound check was stopped mid-flow. Bryan had a headache and was trying to eat his fish and chips in peace with his then girlfriend Vicky Russell, the late Ken Russell's daughter. He was in his dressing room, which was close to the stage. I was furious. I yelled at his tour manager: 'He's eating fish and chips?'

Bryan was a veteran performer, famous and successful in Canada since he was 15-years-old. We were nervous and inexperienced at that level of gig. Plus it was a huge deal for us to be playing Wembley Arena, in London, in our own country as were starting to have hit records. We had a lot to prove. We had a lot riding on that show. I found Bryan later and asked him if that order had really come from him, and asked him if he had any idea how nervous we were and that we only got 15 minutes anyway? He looked uncomfortable and tried to explain he was feeling off his game and needed some quiet time.

After the show he flew on a private plane straight to Switzerland to rest before the next show. We followed like the Ant Hill Mob in our Sharrabang. When we got to Switzerland he took me to one side and gave me a watch he had bought for me at the airport. It was a bit cheap but nevertheless it was an apology.

China In Your Hand reached the number one slot when we were on tour with Bryan Adams. We were in Germany and we knew the single was doing well back home. It was Sunday, chart rundown day, and Jennie went down to the production office to call our management for the UK chart placing. She came back up the stairs, we were all waiting in the corridor with bated breath. She began a chart rundown: 'The Communards are at four, Rick Astley is at number three, George Harrison is at two and YOU are number one!'

We were also number one in the album chart with Bridge Of Spies and the 12-inch mix of China was number one in the Dance chart too. So we were number one on three separate charts simultaneously. We kept George Harrison at number two in the singles chart, and kept Paul

McCartney at number two on the album chart.

We were temporarily bigger than The Beatles! It was quite something. We were screaming! We were bouncing off the walls. Bryan came out of his dressing room looking irritated at the disturbance (not another bloody headache please) and we were all holding up one finger. 'We're number one, we're number one.' Bryan's reaction was to initially be a little perturbed because he wouldn't have wanted to be usurped by his opening act. You don't really want your opening act to be at number one. You want them to be interesting and up-and-coming, and you want them to add to the ticket. But you don't want them to be at number one. After he had processed the info he was great. When that night's show was over, he bought us lots of Champagne and we hung out and partied and played pool. But he was a little uncomfortable with it.

We toured with Bryan for almost three months across Europe and the UK with China In Your Hand doing very well in most places we went. By now we were all getting along with Bryan's band and crew really well. Bryan gave Dean a guitar and Dean was really touched. Tim was big pals with Mickey Curry, Bryan's drummer. Most nights we would be glued to their performance from the wings, in awe of the scale of the gigs, the popularity of the songs and their musical prowess. One night I could not resist trying to put Bryan off by lifting my top and flashing my tits at him. He was in shock for about 10 minutes. I had great tits!

We left 'Into The Fire' and went straight onto our own tour. We had to get used to smaller venues again, but at least they were our own shows.

We were playing at Manchester Apollo, selling out three nights and Bryan was next door playing in the massive MEN Arena. We still had our ITF tour laminates, so we were able to go backstage as usual at his show on our night off. It was weird seeing another support act in our place. I felt territorial: we'd been on tour with him for so long. I was standing by the monitor desk watching him in action, with my tits firmly inside my top, and he called me on to the stage.

The packed Arena went wild when I walked on, I was very well known at home by now. He asked me to duet on 'Run To You' with him. It was a great moment in my career.

China catapulted us into 'The Big Time'. All of a sudden we were getting invited to all sorts of PR events like film premieres, showbiz' awards, trendy club openings and the opening of envelopes. There were a lot of red carpets events with paparazzi snapping away. I had my share of photographers hiding behind parked cars and leaping out at me. But 'papping' wasn't on the scale that it is today.

Our new life was crazy-busy. I felt I had to pinch myself sometimes, but I was starting to make those progressive steps into the world of the famous and I liked it. I liked the recognition and I liked the respect. Don't forget, it had been a long time coming. I started singing in 1981 and didn't start to make my first record for another six years. I felt validated by fame, which I learned at my cost leaves you a very slippery slope as regards your emotional stability.

It wasn't all easy of course, and we found ourselves under more scrutiny than ever before. One thing that I got slated for was my age. I was 28-years-old when I got my record deal.

I have already mentioned Jackie Castellano, our stylist, flagging it up when I was 26.

Mariella Frostrup, the broadcaster and writer, was then part of a company called Ferret and Spanner, the go-to music biz PR company of the day. She looked after many successful artists including us. She quickly sliced a few years off my age. I didn't realise it was a problem. I had never thought about my age in terms of numbers, more in terms of how I felt and how I looked.

I was booked to appear on a 'Yoof' TV program called Network Seven, which was the brainchild of Janet Street Porter. Scary hard-hitting journalist Paul Morley was going to interview me live on the show. As we all chatted before the show aired, Paul told me he was really nervous as he had not done much TV, and this was live and new. I reassured him that I was now a veteran of TV chat and would enjoy talking about what we were up to. It was all grist to the mill. The floor manager counted Paul and us in, and he absolutely annihilated me on live TV for lying about my age. I was 30 by the time China went to number one, so I was positively geriatric for the pop world.

He said: 'Why do you lie about your age?' I said: 'I've never lied about my age, other people seem to want to lie about my age, I never have, I'm 30-years-old.'

He then asked: 'Why do you wear such short skirts? Is it to take everybody's mind off your crap music?'

I felt the colour flood to my face. It was a trap. I had been set up. I had a red hot cup of coffee beside me on set and it was all I could do not to scald the fucker.

That was my first taste of the UK media and press starting to tire of us, and turn on me. Years later I was parking my car on the Finchley Road in London. As I got out, I came face to face with Paul Morley with his young daughter. I said 'hello' and smiled sweetly at his little girl. It was his turn to be mortified and blush.

There were so many 'firsts' in our career. There was the first time to the States, first time on Top Of The Pops, first time on the radio, first time at number one and first time on a private jet! But whatever 'first' it was, one thing stayed the stayed the same – we always used to celebrate it by hitting the booze. It was our drug of choice.

Our first private jet was on standby to take us to Munich, to do the German equivalent of Top Of The Pops. When we got in the jet, it was loaded up with snacks and drink, stowed neatly in the sides of the walls. I was necking back Champagne and the boys were on the beer. It was fun time on the party plane. We got delayed on take-off for a while, then we were airborne and it was around a two-hour flight. After about an hour, with gallons of liquid swishing around in our bladders, we all started to need the loo but there was no toilet on board. Who builds a private jet with no loo? How uncivilised! The guys all peed in empty beer cans. I had to hold it in and could barely walk to the terminal when we got to Munich.

For a while, we were in the middle of a whirlwind. T'Paumania hit Britain and Europe, and I lapped it up. I have since met so many women who said they went to their hairdresser to copy my hairdo, and also many hairdressers who tell me they wanted to kill me because of that. We were always on the TV and we were often on the kids' shows, like Going Live, Number 73, as well as Wogan and other music programmes. Our church was broad. At one point I was on the cover of Kerrang!, Melody Maker, Q Magazine, NME, Smash Hits and Number One. I was called 'Springsteen in a split skirt'.

There'd be cameras flicking wherever I went. In the spring of 1988, we were performing at the Montreux Jazz Festival in Switzerland. I got a telephone call from our Mariella to say that the press had been snooping around, interrogating my friends in Shrewsbury.

Annie, a good friend of mine who I'd worked with at Jean Jeanie, in Shrewsbury, had called our management to say that two hacks from The News Of The World's supplement, The Sunday Magazine, had been going around shops, bars and cafes trying to find out who knew me. They said they wanted to do a nice 'rags to riches' piece on me, but my savvy friend didn't believe them. The hacks were Piers Morgan and another female journalist. They were trying to persuade people I knew to talk to them by saying 'we all love Carol and we want to do a background piece about how well she's done' when, in fact, they were trying to dig up any dirt they could find. It was just too good to be true it seemed.

I didn't really have any skeletons in the closet. I'd never been a drug taker, I'd had a couple of boyfriends but they were loyal and closed-mouthed. The only person who spoke to them was Hilda – the landlady at The Three Fishes, where I'd worked. She had been very, very jealous of me and was always putting me down and taking the piss out of me. In the article, she said I painted my Doc Marten's different colours to try and make myself seem special. WOW! Oh and her husband had had me over the barrels downstairs in the cellar of the pub, which simply wasn't true.

Next they went to my mother's house, in Nuneaton. My father was working away in Saudi at the time. Piers showed her his NUJ card and she thought that meant he was kosher. So she let him in, made him his lunch and then spent the afternoon nattering away to him, showing him my baby pictures and filling him in on how I'd been as a teenager. When the article was published it turned out to be a very badly written hatchet piece and my mother was in tears on the phone. She said: 'I would never have spoken to him but they told me they were going to do a lovely article on how you'd made it big.' When my friends and family read it they were just devastated, and felt as though they, and I, had been stitched up. It had so little substance to it that Mariella said that I was either the most boring person in the world or I had the most loyal friends.

At the 1988 BPI (now the BRIT Awards), Piers swaggered over to our table, stooped down and put his arm around my shoulders and basically said: 'No hard feelings, you know how it is, I was just doing my job.' I said I may be fair game but my Mum was not, and could he please piss off. He continued to try to justify what he'd done. Our normally mild-mannered A&R man, Simon, stood up and very John Wayne-like said: 'I think the lady asked you to leave.' Piers skulked off unforgiven.

The 1988 BPIs were our first major awards ceremony. We had been nominated for five:

Best Single

Best Album

Best newcomer

Best Video

Best International Breakthrough artist

We did not pick up one of them.

I was later told that it's all a bit incestuous and that a lot of the industry did not like Richard Branson or Virgin, and were sick of T'Pau so they voted politically. Years later, when I was on the voting panel for the Ivor Novello Awards, I witnessed that first hand. Some of the judges did not vote on the music. They had prejudices and personal jealousies.

Maybe we were a casualty of this, as I fail to see how we could have dominated the charts for the previous 12 months and not been given at least one of those awards.

We opened the Awards at The Albert Hall. It was packed to the rafters with 5,000 people, including all the industry big wigs and huge stars like U2. I had to walk down a huge flight of stairs singing China live in front of my peers. It was nerve wracking, but we got an ovation so we were buzzing. The after-show dinner was at The Grosvenor House Hotel on Park Lane. It was very swanky. The awards then were much more intimate. I think these days, it is too cavernous and impersonal at The O2 Arena. We were sharing our table with Fergal Sharkey from

The Undertones and getting on like a house on fire. He was a top laugh. On the table next to us were The Cure. Ronnie and I were both huge fans. They wrote brilliant pop songs and made very cool videos. They, however, were not fans of ours. Their bass player had viciously slagged off China in a singles review. They were glaring at us and started to throw bread, so we started to throw it back and it was all getting a bit alcohol-fuelled and nasty. Fergal stood up and shouted over: 'What the fuck is the problem with The Adams Family?' He was ready for a fight. We were all calmed down by our various record company people, but it still makes me sad that I love their music and bought their records and they despised us.

In between fights and arguments with The Cure and Piers Morgan, Richard Branson came over to our table with Ken Berry, who was running Virgin Records for him. Virgin owned Siren Records, our label. Richard congratulated Ronnie and I on the success we'd achieved for ourselves, and also thanked us for what we'd achieved for Virgin, which is pretty funny when you think we had that rejection letter from Virgin on the day we signed to Siren. Feeling buoyed up by wine, I felt a little cheeky and said: 'Well if you're that grateful, how about a free holiday on your Island?' We all laughed and chatted for a while then they went off to 'work the room'. On Monday morning, Chris Cooke called me and said Richard's office had called him and asked when I wanted to go! We flew out to Necker Island on the 1st September 1988 for two weeks; I celebrated my 31st birthday there.

Necker Island is the most beautiful perfect jewel in the Caribbean; it is a very personal place to Richard Branson. It is his home and we were privileged to be taken there. But I don't think we realised it enough at the time as we were getting used to being spoilt. In 1988 It was a simple-but-lovely open plan pagoda-shaped house with no glass windows .The shutters peeled right back so that you were almost in the open. Lizards ran around the house. It had a large dining area with a huge baronial table and chairs, pool table, card and reading area, infinity pool and two Jacuzzis. A full staff and a motor launch were at our disposal.

The main building was built of stone and timber with a thatched roof. It was very simple and luxurious all at once. Since the fire in 2011, it has all been rebuilt to be very slick but Necker Mark One was very special.

Ronnie and I invited RBT and his wife Terri, Dean Howard and his wife Gill, and friends from London and Shrewsbury. The day we arrived, the entire staff were lined up on the jetty to welcome us. As we all stepped onto the jetty China In Your Hand was booming through speakers. It was slightly embarrassing being 'piped' ashore with our own song. Cocktails were ready for us. Ronnie and I had Richard's suite upstairs, away from the rest of the house. It had its own balcony and private Jacuzzi. The pace on Necker was very slow. One of my friends said she found the constant 'sshhh sshhh sshh' sound of the staff dragging their feet in flip-flops on the stone floor irritating. After one day in that heat, we were all dragging ours.

At night we would play pool and cards, watch videos, we danced a lot, laughed a lot and drank gallons of Champagne, wine, cocktails and Red Stripe beer. Some people liked a little smoke too, if you get my drift. It was the right part of the world to get it after all. In the morning everyone would emerge bleary eyed for the huge breakfast selection on the terrace.

Mornings were spent swimming, jacuzzy-ing, rubbing on suntan lotion, turning over on our sunbeds, chatting, reading and possibly having an early pina colada. Boy, it was exhausting!

The housekeeper would then ask me, as head of the party, if we wanted lunch on the terrace, or a BBQ lunch on the beach, or would we like a buffet on the launch: oh God such decisions so early! Life was hard. We took the launch out several times to various islands and coves.

After a boozy lunch one day, I dived off the boat into a shoal of Barracuda, not knowing that they are more vicious than sharks and attack people more frequently.

Luckily they had been fed a lot by all the people on the boats so were full. I was yanked back into the boat unharmed, and ticked off by the Captain.

Roy's wife Terri had been raised in California and was a superb water skier. She had been a model and actress. She was typically Californian, tanned, leggy and blonde. She emerged daily with full make-up, beautifully groomed flowing highlighted honey-blonde hair, wearing all her jewellery and her watch. She got on a mono ski in ankle deep water, skied around the bay, let go of the rope and glided back into ankle deep water and gingerly stepped off her ski bone dry. When I water ski, I get an ugly middle parting in my hair that makes me look depressed, have seaweed between my teeth and have to do a lot of bikini bottom retrieving.

Most afternoons it rained a lot, and pools of fresh water on the ground and in the palms of the giant Aloe leaves created a breeding ground for mosquitoes. We all got bitten to death. I woke up one morning and really thought I had gone blind. I could not see at all! I reached out and shook Ronnie, who was asleep next to me. I was panicking and crying. Ronnie said: 'It's OK, don't panic, you've been bitten on your eyelids and they have swollen shut.'

We got some antihistamines and the housekeeper got poultices to bathe my eyes open.

I reacted very badly to the mosquito bites. We counted 300 bites on Malcolm's legs. They were tiny red pinpricks. He had no reaction at all. Everybody else had a bump or two, whereas I looked like the Elephant Man!

Of course the reason for all the heavy rain and by now rising winds was that Hurricane Gilbert was coming our way. The staff were now having to close the shutters. The house rattled and creaked like a wooden ship at sea. Paradise suddenly became a bit scary and we started to feel vulnerable, as the house was right on the top of a tiny island. Sadly our holiday was cut short, as we had to be evacuated to the mainland before the storm hit.

We did have a very a scary and perilous boat ride across to Beef Island to catch a flight out, but at least we got out in time. Hurricane Gilbert went on to be the most powerful tropical cyclone and hurricane in history in the Atlantic basin, devastating the Caribbean and Mexican coastline. Ronnie and I went to Jamaica in 1992 and the island still had not recovered. Mariella Frostrup, our PR, jumped on this as an opportunity to make out to the press that we were almost lost at sea.

Bridge Of Spies was an enormous record. It spawned five top 20 singles, including China In Your Hand, and reached quadruple platinum status, selling 2.5 million copies in the UK alone. We toured for close on 17 months around Europe. And as that era ended, it was time to make another record. The expectation was enormous. We and the label decided to renew our partnership with RTB. We recorded in several studios, including the now-defunct Olympic, in Barnes, owned by Richard Branson. It had a very corporate, hotel-like dark blue patterned foyer carpet. At a subsequent party at Richard's house in Oxfordshire, I couldn't help but notice he had it in his house too. Rich but thrifty, he must have got a job lot.

I always had the greatest admiration and respect for Richard. He has always been most generous to me and remained so long after our association with him ended. When a distant cousin of mine was sadly dying of cancer in Hong Kong, we were having a whip round to raise money, as her parents could not afford the flight. I called Richard's PA to see if we could get a discounted rate. He flew them out first class on Virgin to be by her side free of charge.

We started recording Rage, our second album, at Wisseloord Studios in Hilversum, in Holland, just one hour from s-'Hertogenbosch where I had worked in that bar a decade ago. T'Pau had done very well in Holland; China had been at number one there for three weeks.

I got recognised most places I went and was very proud that my photo was put up on the wall in the rogues' gallery of famous guests at the prestigious American Hotel, in Amsterdam. I was hanging proudly in the main bar in 1988. On a return visit in 2010, I had travelled down the corridor and was heading for the toilet, usurped down the years by more current faces. Ah well, that's showbiz.

Wisseloord contained three huge state of the art studios. Def Leppard were in one with Mutt Lange. There was a very nice artists' café and lounge, which made the studio very sociable, so it wasn't long before we were on a very friendly footing with The Leps'. Joe Elliott and I kept in touch for a while later.

In the other studio was Greek icon Nana Mouskouri. One morning,

I had gone into the café to get a coffee, no staff were there so I nipped behind the bar to make my own. Nana came walking in and smiled sweetly, she asked for a cappuccino, no sugar. She thought I worked there. I laughed inwardly and decided not to correct her. I made her coffee, asked her if she took sugar, and she took her coffee and went back to her studio. It was so funny.

Many years later I was recording my album, Red, in The Roundhouse Studios, in London. I was heavily pregnant with Scarlett and it was about 11pm. I was knackered and my back was aching. I went to the kitchen/lounge and a young skinny boy was lying on the sofa watching TV. Presuming he was the night desk guy, I asked could he make me a cup of tea and flopped down in front of the TV as well. He made me a lovely cuppa' and we chatted for a while. My guitarist came out of the studio to get me for a vocal take and asked in excited tones: 'How did you get chatting to Fran Healey, was he nice?'

The guy making my cuppa had been the lead singer of Travis, who were massive at that time. I had said nothing to Nana and Fran said nothing to me. I wonder if he had spent many years as a waiter as well?

The recording of Rage was a little trickier. We had changed sound engineer as Jerry Napier, although a brilliant engineer, was a truculent person. On a couple of occasions, when we were all pissed he made it clear to me that he fancied me. I did not feel the same and I only had eyes for Ronnie. He then, in my opinion, felt foolish that he had revealed this to me and was odd with me ever after. I told Ronnie that after we had finished the album and he didn't want Jerry back either.

Jerry had also been really bitchy behind Roy's back and we idolised Roy at that time, so one night I spilled those beans and Roy fired him.

We had worked with several engineers over the years now and we chose Norman Goodman. Norman was a great engineer and a very funny guy, but he and Roy did not get always get along. Norman had different ways of achieving sounds and effects – Roy had his extravagant crazy methods and was not happy if Norman pointed out there was a more efficient way of doing something. He took it as criticism. Jerry helped Roy achieve what he wanted. Norman would question things but only for the good of the record/budget.

However, looking back, maybe it wasn't his place to do that. His job was to simply press the buttons. But I also think Roy was pissed off not to bring his own person, and determined to be awkward with whoever was thrust upon him. Ronnie and I also had many production ideas and a lot to say on Rage. We had matured and now had a lot more experience. Our success had given us confidence in our own ideas. Roy was often quite quiet in the control room. His wife, Terri, told me later that Roy felt we didn't need him. We did but we had more of a contribution to make. But sadly things were not the same as they were.

We did however make a great album. The band were tight as musicians and as friends. Dean Howard had now been our lead guitarist for a year. Taj had left to join Julia Fordham to get his jazz rocks off shortly after the Nik Kershaw tour. Michael, of course, could still have a moan-fest, and the bitchy wives would pitch up now and again to whinge. But mainly things were good between us. We moved around three or four studios to complete Rage. Virgin America did not like the mixes we did and insisted we remixed the album for North America and Canada. We also had to have another cover shot for them as they didn't understand the European one. All those adjustments went on our bill, of course.

We went to The Manor outside Oxford to remix the album with Gary Lagan, ex-Art Of Noise.

It was a beautiful stone 16th century Manor House. Due to being listed it had no air-conditioning. The studio was in a converted stone barn beside the main house. At that time, let's just say several personnel enjoyed 'wacky baccy'. I have never really smoked marijuana. I tried it but did not take to it. Due to the lack of aircon', you could almost cut the air with a knife and step through it. After an evening of sitting in the control room I would go hunting for biscuits and chocolate. It took me a while to figure out I had the passive munchies.

We took a day off and Ronnie, Dean and I went shopping, and I got absolutely mobbed. I couldn't get out of the shop. Ronnie just melted into the background and I was really upset with him. I felt he didn't protect me. Dean stood by me as I signed endless autographs (there were no mobile cameras then) and eventually he said: 'Sorry folks I have to get her back to the studio now.' We had to cut our shopping trip short. When I asked Ronnie why he left me so vulnerable he replied: 'I don't want to spend the rest of my life standing in shop doorways while you sign bits of paper.' That really hurt me. I realised the schism was beginning.

The price of fame was taking its toll on us.

With the album finished, we began our 'Rage Across Europe Tour'. Now it was our turn to play the arenas .We had our own stage set built with ramps and walkways and huge mesh fencing all around. We had a really top class crew. Tom Kenny was our lighting designer. Steve Levitt was our front of house. Those guys were, and still are, hugely sought after. We had the late great choreographer Bob Talmadge, son of Buster Keaton, flown in from LA to teach us how to work a big stage: we tended to have stage agorophobia and huddle in one spot, having always been short on space as the opening act. He worked us into the floor, running the show from top to bottom about six times a day.

We took over The St Austell Coliseum, which is sadly now gone, for a week of production rehearsals. We did our first gig there to kick off the tour and the video for Road To Our Dream up the coast at Tintagel. We camped out at the beautiful Foye Hotel. We worked hard and played very hard.

Rage Across Europe took us . . . across Europe! We now got to headline the big arenas in the UK including London Wembley, Newcastle Metro, Glasgow SECC and Birmingham NEC. At the NEC, a decision was made to bring the stage time forward by 15 minutes. The band was told by Jennie. The FOH and lighting engineers had also been informed but nobody told the stage crew.

We took our places side of stage, the house lights went down and the roar of the crowd went up. The band went on and fired up Sex Talk. They had no monitors at all. They couldn't hear a thing and were all glancing around in wide-eyed confusion. It was planned that I stalk onto the stage in time for the first verse. I was confronted with a mic stand with no mic on it! Looking desperately around I saw my radio mic in pieces, drying out from being disinfected and there was no monitor engineer in sight.

The band went round the intro for the fourth time, and by then the crowd was looking confused. It was another Spinal Tap moment. Moose, our monitor engineer, came sprinting from his desk in catering, which was no mean feat as he was not a slip of a lad. Frantically, he started to assemble my mic. Realising it was just too messy a start to our blockbuster-of-a-show, I looked at Tim our drummer and gave him the cut-throat sign to stop the song. Moose raced on stage with my mic, looking terrified. I addressed a packed NEC and said: 'This is what we call in the industry a 'fuck up'.The whole venue laughed and cheered and we started Sex Talk again, finishing it to a standing ovation. When we played Glasgow SECC, which has several huge concert halls, The Care Bears had sold out the bigger venue.

The Two Dianas

The world's most famous woman at that time was Princess Diana. And our paths crossed on more than one occasion. Let me rewind, first of all, to 1983 and one July evening, not too late, around 9pm.

I've already told you a little about when Ronnie and I were out drinking in Soho. We found ourselves near where Oxford Street meets Tottenham Court Road. We could see that about 200 yards away to our right, a huge throng of people had gathered outside the Dominion Theatre. They were spilling across the road and being moved back by the traffic police.

We approached the action and I asked someone what was going on. It was the Prince's Trust Concert and the main artist attraction was Duran Duran. The person people really wanted to see, however, was the Princess of Wales. I managed to balance on the railings and hold on to a lamppost. A huge shiny black car glided to a smooth halt outside the theatre and the myriad of camera flashbulbs that went off turned the night sky to day.

From my precarious perch I saw the Prince of Wales and Diana. Getting caught up in the excitement, I waved and cheered, and Charles looked straight at me and waved back. I don't usually go in for crowd hysterics, I find them peculiar, but even I got caught up in the moment.

Of course he didn't recognise me from our brief meeting in Ironbridge all those years ago, I knew it was just an accidental locking of eyes. Then Diana got out of the car and the flash bulbs went crazy. To view first-hand the press attention she received was intimidating and jaw-droppingly awesome.

Diana was by now a global superstar. You know, it's a phrase we've all come to loathe because of that blasted TV show, The X Factor, but she had it in spades. People used to look down their nose at her and I was dismissive too. The press joked that she was stupid because she wasn't academic. She'd been a chalet girl, a cleaner and a nanny. Looking back that was quite cruel. She had a lovely natural light touch with people, something that you can't get a degree in. Besides, she was also really quite shy.

But Diana had many other qualities, too, and I am here to tell you that she was very sweet and very funny. When you were in her presence she radiated charm. In conversation, she focused on the person she was talking to, making them feel like the most important person in the world. She had an incredible aura too and she also had great natural beauty. In the flesh, with those sapphire blue eyes and that slight Mona Lisa smile, she'd light up any room. Not many pictures really captured that when she was young. She went on to develop her own immaculate style, but when the world first discovered her she had a bit of a basin haircut and a big conk. Top photographer Mario Testino captured her incredible maturing beauty in the last shots he took of her for Vanity Fair shortly before she died. They were poignant photographs and she looked beautiful, relaxed and comfortable in her own skin.

The perceived wisdom was that she was finally happy. To die so soon afterwards was a cruel twist of fate.

But outside The Dominion that night as part of the crowd, I couldn't know that it would only be six years later that I would be performing with

T'Pau at The Prince's Trust Gala and rubbing shoulders with the Princess.

When that day came, I was elated. Being a part of such a high-level industry gig was a great coup and by then we were on such a roll that such occasions were becoming routine. Yeah, so Chuck and Di would be there, but I had never particularly bothered with the Royals. I am not anti-monarchy, but to me they were just there, part of British tradition, I had no real interest in them.

I had not yet met Diana and had not been caught up in the growing fascination with her: she was the shy, eyelash-fluttering, dim Sloane married to crusty old Charles. Prior to meeting her, I rather thought that it would be a huge thrill for her to meet me, to bask in the reflected glory of my rock band! I had to be more interesting than that dreary middle-aged mob she had married into. In fact, I was so involved in my own little world that I didn't really notice much outside my own growing fame, which I was enjoying immensely and I assumed everyone else was too.

The Prince's Trust Gala concert was to be held at the London Palladium in April 1989. As a child I remembered the TV show, Sunday Night At The Palladium. It was a blast to tread the boards of such a venerable establishment. We had to get there by 10am and we stayed all day to do copious rehearsals and photo shoots.

As it was a small theatre and a large cast, we had to share dressing rooms, which are often poky in theatres; at least the one I got always was.

I was in what appeared to be a prison cell with Marie Helvin, the famous model, and Sandra Bernhard, the famous lesbian comedienne. She had lately gained notoriety by 'lezzing' it up with Madonna, and I knew her only from her reputation as an aggressive, mouthy, rude, not-very-funny-at-all American.

I was first in the room and bagged a small table by the window. Sandra entered next; clearly horrified by the shabby room she had to share with people she had never heard of, her being, as I said, such a famous lesbian. I looked at her in my mirror, my reflection starting a welcoming smile and was about to say 'hello' when she blurted out: 'Hi, I'm Sandra, you stay outta my hair and I'll stay outta yours.' My jaw dropped. 'Excuse me?' I asked. 'Only joking,' she retreated slightly, and began to fuss about her gown with her assistant. She wasn't joking.

Marie Helvin came into the room. She said a very nice 'hello' to me and sort of glowered at Sandra, who ignored her right back. I did not know what was going on there. It was the most hostile dressing room vibe I have ever experienced.

Jerry Hall was introducing T'Pau on stage that night. As a young follower of fashion, I remembered almost every magazine cover that she and her good friend Marie Helvin had adorned. I felt like a dwarf in a production of Snow White. Was there a dwarf called Insignificant? Those two tall slender beauties had been my heroines growing up in Shropshire. I love fashion, make-up and magazines and when I was young I had written her a fan letter. I'd been a teenager at the time and she'd had the grace to write back to me, though I didn't tell her that on that day.

In the '70s and '80s they knew EVERYONE; they went EVERYWHERE – and here I was squashed in prison with them. Jerry had come sulking into our room as she had to share with the teenage American starlet Debbie Gibson and Debbie's mum would not let Jerry smoke. Jerry came to ours for a ciggie. She moved to smoke out of the window and as I had the table by the window she had to lean right over me. I inhaled her perfume and nicotine like a drug. Maybe if I breathed in her fumes I would grow taller and more beautiful. Those women, and not Diana, made me tongue-tied and gauche. They had been famous for aeons.

When Sandra popped out, Jerry and Marie told me that she was vile and they didn't like her. So I thought I had better not like her either. Truth was, she was sort of fascinating merely because she was so astonishingly rude. Her tongue-in-cheek lesbo' version of Me And Mrs Jones was later cut from the TV production of the show because it was too racy!

The concert on that occasion was more like a variety show than a rock show. There were many different sorts of entertainers on the bill, including Dame Kiri Te Kanawa, the world-famous Antipodean soprano and real, actual Dame Of The Realm. There were also comedians like Lenny Henry and Dame Edna Everage, the world-famous Aussie 'housewife-superstar' and not actually a Dame Of The Realm but

comedian Barry Humphries. We approached showtime and completed
our final dress rehearsal including all of us lining up on the stage for a
practice finale.

It was a packed stage and the theatre staircase leading back to the
dressing rooms was extremely narrow so we were held in a long celebrity
queue; there could be a TV show there. There then began an ushering of
and a fussing around the more high-brow artists by the concert staff.

Someone behind me announced loudly: 'Excuse us, make way
please and allow Dame Kiri and Dame Edna through, yes, thank you step
aside please.' We were gently moved aside as both Grand Dames swept
through. I could not help myself and I shouted out, pointing at Barry
Humphries: 'But he's not a real Dame, he's not even a real woman. It's
an Australian bloke in a frock!' I confess, I may have had a glass of wine
by then. It was all to no avail. Barry took advantage of the situation, and
without a glimmer of guilt in his eye disappeared up the stairs. I think that
in-character he'd also forgotten that he wasn't a real Dame.

I did however then get the opportunity to pinch Lenny Henry's bum
as he slowly climbed the stairs ahead of me.

Wet Wet Wet were playing the show too but they were really late
for the rehearsals. The organisers were starting to have kittens by the
time they arrived because it was a live show to a packed theatre of very
posh jewellery-rattlers, who were due in their seats within the hour.
When I asked Wet Wet Wet singer Marti Pellow what had happened,
he swaggered back that they had been at a label party to pick up their
'Multi-Tulti-Ulti-eth platinum album.' Marti was, back then, just a tad
egomaniacal, always trying to rub it in as he definitely saw us as direct
competition. I, on the other hand preferred not to compare us to their,
albeit-massively-successful, pub-band sound.

Just before her performance Mica Paris had a broken microphone and
we helpfully offered her the use of my radio mic. She swiped it out of my
hand like I was the help and flounced onto the stage without a word of
thanks. She was not in a very good mood but was also way too big and
too rock-hard to be pulled up on her manners. In fact, I think I thanked
her for handing it back. Jerry Hall took her place on the stage and began

to read our little introductory biog from the distant autocue. Unfortunately due to being either myopic or just from Texas she stumbled over almost every syllable and finally introduced us as Tee Paw.

For the show I had insisted on performing a lively but not very well-known album track called Taking Time Out, as it was getting boring only ever performing China In Your Hand at such events. I didn't realise at the time what a stupid idea it was to deliberately avoid our most prestigious track; I'd got a bad dose of misguided artistic petulance. We executed it well enough but the audience looked bemused and felt short-changed, and I knew as I sang I had made the wrong call. It was one of many. Rewind please. Can I have another go at it all?

After the concert Ronnie and I had to get in the line-up in the upper reception area to be presented to the dignitaries, while the rest of the band stood down. I always want to giggle on stuffy occasions. At Holy Communion I'd try not to choke on the bread, or waiting outside the beak's office at school I'd try to look penitent. At funerals, I'd always try to look upset. But in any situation where you should not laugh, I always get inappropriate laughter. It's probably nerves.

Sean Connery was presenting all the artists to Charles and Diana. He had to remind Charles who was who and what they had just done. Diana could remember everybody without a prompt. They approached slowly and I looked at the floor to try to regain some composure. Charles arrived in front of Ron and I and somebody whispered our description to Sean, who duly whispered it to Charles: 'T'Pau, Your Highness.'

Prince Charles enquired through characteristically clenched teeth: 'What exactly is that?'

'I'm a singer, Your Highness. I was just on the stage, I sang for you – with a band?'

Desperately trying to jar his memory. He guffawed and pretended to remember. I wasn't fooled. If only we'd played China, he would've forgotten everyone else. Damn.

I had decided that I would not curtsy and I didn't. I shook hands vigorously. To me the curtsy is the gesture of an inferior, a serf, and although it was really interesting to meet them, I did not feel that I was their inferior. In fact, as I explained earlier, I was feeling at the time immensely superior to most people.

Diana shuffled behind him, shaking various hands. As she approached, I suddenly remembered that she had just had her wisdom teeth out, so I asked whether she was in pain, knowing from personal experience how much it hurts when they are impacted and the dentist has to put his knee on your chest to yank 'em out. 'Not too bad, thanks,' she replied. 'I looked like a hamster until yesterday.' Sweet, I think.

After the formalities were over everyone decamped to the reception area for a drink and Charles and Diana began to circulate more casually. The whole of T'Pau and various wives were standing in a circle chatting when I felt a gentle but powerful presence behind me. Those opposite me suddenly grinned from ear to ear and nodded at me. I turned around to find Diana waiting politely for a break in our conversation. She had yet to develop into the fashion icon that she later became. That night she was wearing a bright yellow satin two-piece skirt-suit and looked a bit like a very pretty banana. I made space for her in our circle and she stepped forward and asked how we had enjoyed the show. I joked that I couldn't see many young faces in the audience. Diana playfully admonished me, 'Hey, I'm young!' She was only 27.

Diana was so tall – far taller than I expected. In the flesh, she was incredibly attractive. Those blue eyes blazed from her head. I had never seen a picture in the papers that conveyed the mischievous twinkle in those eyes and unless you talked with her you couldn't know that she was charming, witty and sharp. The papers always undersold her as the Sloane with an O Level in looking after hamsters, or something like that.

As I said I am not overly bothered about the monarchy, I'm neither pro- or anti-. Dean Howard, our diamond-in-the-rough guitarist, however, was quite vehement in his dislike of them. 'Useless, sponging wankers. The French had the right idea, cut their heads off and get rid of the lot of them.' But even for him the Diana Effect kicked in, and he had a gormless mile-wide smile. 'Oi Di!' He elbowed her in the ribs to get her attention. I swear to GOD this is just as it happened. Diana looked at me and gave a wry little grin. I shook my head and looked at the floor. 'I'm off to the bar,' he continued. 'Can I get you a drink?'

'An orange juice would be great, thanks,' replied The Princess.

''Ow's about a little nip o' vodka in that?'

'I'd love to, but I'd better not, thanks – still on duty.'

Dean went off to the bar and Diana chatted easily with the rest of the band. On his return he handed her an OJ. 'There you go love.'

Diana smiled at him, took her drink with thanks and said she had better circulate. She went off sipping it. I remember thinking: 'God, some nutter could've poisoned her so easily.' Nobody intercepted the drink at all.

I teased Dean about his hypocrisy. He said he still had no time for them but declared Diana 'alright'. Praise indeed.

At a subsequent Prince's Trust photo shoot, the photographer uttered that usual cliché and told us all to say cheese. Diana turned to me and whispered: 'Say bitch – you get a much sexier smile.'

I have never forgotten the tip.

We played two shows for the Prince and I've got letters from Charles thanking me for performing – it's not a bad return for a girl who he mistook for being someone from borstal all those years before.

The first letter said:

Dear Miss Decker,

I just wanted to write and say how touched I was that you felt able to take part in the recent Prince's Trust Gala at the London Palladium. It was extremely generous of you and I can't tell you how much I appreciated such a kind gesture. Apart from anything else I really enjoyed the contribution you made on stage and I thought the whole evening was a stunning, professional success. As a result of your participation we will be able to help many more young people achieve their potential, and that is what really matters.

This brings you my warmest thanks and best wishes.

Yours sincerely, Charles

On the next occasion, he wrote:

Dear Miss Decker,

I wanted to write and say how enormously grateful I am to you for taking the trouble to perform in that splendid rock concert in the Albert Hall the other evening. Knowing how many demands there are on your time makes me even more appreciative of such a generous gesture to my Trust. I still can't believe that so many stars are prepared to come together and play in one band on yet another occasion. This year the results were even more spectacular than before and my wife and I really enjoyed the music you all produced. It was still ringing in our ears for some time afterwards!

This brings you renewed thanks and my very best wishes.

Yours sincerely, Charles

The Prince's Trust events were among the best. Everybody who was anybody would be there: it was like Rock Star Boot Camp. At one of the galas, I met George Harrison, Roger Daltrey, Eric Clapton and Elton John. Sir Elton specifically asked to be introduced to me.

After the show, we'd gathered in a huge room to enjoy a buffet. Somebody tapped me on the shoulder and said: 'Elton would like to meet you.' So I turned round and could see Elton marching towards me. I was thinking: 'Fucking hell, it's Elton John.' I put my hand straight out to shake his hand, but Elton put his arms out to showbiz-hug me. It was a classic case of when-two-worlds-collide and my outstretched hand ended up punching him straight in the stomach, which was really embarrassing. He recovered from the winding I gave him and congratulated me on our success.

I had a similar clumsy encounter on another occasion with a different rock legend. The fantastically-famous guitarist Jeff Beck came to our show at the Hammersmith Odeon. We shared a tour manager, Al Dutton, who told me: 'Jeff's up in the bar and he'd really like to meet you.' So I made my way to the very grimy backstage bar and I stepped forward to shake hands. As I walked towards Jeff, I slipped on a slice of lemon that had been dropped onto the floor. I skidded forward and started to fall, just about managing to stop myself from hitting the floor by grabbing onto Jeff's belt buckle. As my motion ended, I found myself almost on my knees, hands around his belt buckle with my face in his crotch. It was the first time we'd met. Jeff said: 'My, you are pleased to meet me aren't you?'

I met Jeff again in 2014 at a party and he remembered me. He said: 'I remember you falling over and putting your face in my balls.' Having not seen him for so long I asked if he fancied lunch sometime. My husband is the executive chef of a group of BBQ restaurants in London. So I said to Jeff and his wife: 'You guys have toured The States so many times, don't you just love the BBQ food out there, the pulled pork, the wings and burnt ends, would you like to be my guest at Bodeans?' Jeff replied, coolly that they had both been vegetarians for over 40 years. EEEEK. It was my second Jeff Beck faux pas. I will just keep out of his way, I think.

As well as Elton, I met Roger Daltrey and George Harrison waved at me. The two of them were talking and they hailed me over to chat, shaking my hand. George teased me about keeping his song 'Got My Mind Set On You' at number two in the charts.

As much as I enjoyed meeting them, I remember at the time not being able to get over the fact that I was hanging out with a Beatle and the singer from The Who. I just couldn't get over it. I felt like an imposter. The giants in the industry were taking time out to say hello to little old me. And they were so nice and normal and chatty. I quaked in my boots and was absolutely honoured they spent a little time with me. I felt as though I was flying.

But alas not everyone was fun. What's the saying? Never meet your heroes.

One of the most disappointing experiences in my career so far – though there's always room for another – was meeting Diana Ross. I had been raised listening to her voice. My parents had all the Motown hits, including The Motown Story, an amazing box set of vinyl albums with tracks from all the artists plus dialogue from Berry Gordy and various managers and Tamla artists. I was one of millions of fans who loved The Supremes, particularly the waif-like Diana Ross. She looked to me like a black Audrey Hepburn, a fine-boned, delicate beauty. She had a unique voice. She was also a very good actress, getting an Oscar nomination for her harrowing portrayal of Billie Holiday in Lady Sings The Blues. Her career was pure gold for many years.

But it had been rumoured over the years that this fragile bird of a girl was quite ruthlessly ambitious. I had read the unofficial biography, Call Her Miss Ross, which painted a picture of the ultimate diva, clawing her way up from a tough inner-city life in The Projects in Detroit, to the top of the tree, using both her tremendous talent and also her feminine attributes.

In 1995, to commemorate the Halifax Rugby League Centenary, I was asked to record a song with appropriately uplifting 'we can do it!' lyrics. It was called One Heart and we were to perform it on the hallowed turf of Wembley Stadium.

Diana Ross was also on the bill. I couldn't wait. I was shown to my lovely dressing room, which was a small suite. Diana's was next door. Her assistant Estelle came to my dressing room and said 'hi'. She told me to just ask if I needed anything. 'How sweet! This is all going to be so cosy!' I thought.

I was called to do my sound check and we ran the track a few times to get the monitors right, so that I could hear myself. We were performing on a small square stage right in the centre of the pitch and I felt like an ant. I have sold out Wembley Arena, which I believe holds around 12,500 souls and that was a thrilling achievement. But to play in our most famous stadium was something unique. The sheer scale of the event was almost overwhelming. I imagined how it must provide the biggest adrenaline rush for our football and rugby players. By the time I returned to my dressing room, Diana Ross was in hers. The door was ajar and a big bodyguard was planted outside.I went into my room with my management and guitarist Dougie, stopping to chat to Estelle and ask if Diana would like to meet. Our conversation was cut short by Estelle's name being screamed out. 'ESTELLE! Where are my gold shoes? Estelle!'

Estelle gave me a limp smile and called back: 'Coming Miss Ross.'

So it was true! You did have to call her Miss Ross. The walls were quite thin and we could her shrieking constantly at her poor PA. No wonder Estelle was trying to hang with us. After about an hour there was a knock on my door and a rugby official told us that Diana was 'ready to meet us now'. I was a little irritated to be summoned but I was still madly curious to meet her. There was a line-up of dignitaries and players, and me. It was just like being at The Prince's Trust. We had to stand in line to meet Diana Ross, as though she was royalty. She behaved as though she was The Other Diana. I couldn't believe it! Why were we all doing this?

Eventually she got to me and I said: 'Hi Diana, pleasure to meet you. I'm Carol; I'm a singer too. I was just sound checking a little while ago.' Through her famous and massive white perma-smile, Diana said only: 'Yes, I heard you…' It was the ultimate put down. Then she moved on to the next person. It cut like a knife. A few months before I'd seen her turn in an excellent Golden Globe-winning performance in a TV movie about a schizophrenic called 'Out Of Darkness', and I wanted to congratulate her, and also make a last ditch attempt to get her to talk to me. So I blurted out: 'By the way Diana …' I never got to finish my sentence. The withering look that she shot me across her shoulder shut me straight up. I had had my turn; who was I to try to approach her without permission? And I did not even call her Miss Ross.

I sang my song to a pretty good reaction from the rugger crowd, then Status Quo also played and they brought the house down.

Diana wore a gold lamé cape and was driven in an open-top Rolls Royce Silver Ghost around the perimeter of the pitch, miming out of sync and waving regally to the little people. The bemused crowd of big tough rugby fans gave her a very tepid reception; she went down like a fart in a spaceship. But the next day her picture was splashed across all the front pages of The Tabloids and she received huge praise. I don't think The Quo and I even got a mention. Ah well, that's showbiz.

Dirty Laundry

Our years at Pengwern didn't come to an end immediately. It's funny, but when you've had a number one, you can still be quite skint. People imagine that if you're at number one, a huge truck filled with money pulls up outside your house and you're suddenly rich. But that doesn't happen.

We eventually got paid for our hits, but it took quite a while for those funds to come through. In fact, we didn't end up leaving Shrewsbury permanently until late 1988. Ronnie and I were spending so much time in London, and I loved it so much that I pushed for us to move thinking it was what we both wanted. Malcolm Rigby, a good friend of ours based in London, helped us find the right house. We needed enough space to install a recording studio and we also wanted to be close to the centre of town so that we could have fun! We found a three-storey, slightly clapped-out Victorian town house on Chetwynd Road, in Tufnell Park, right around the corner from The Forum, where we had gigged with Nik Kershaw. It was a spit from the Tube and the scruffy end of Hampstead Heath. It had plenty of space and a small garden. It was a great find for the price. The house was owned by a family of five. We knocked on the door. When it opened the children looked at me in wide-eyed amazement. We toured the house and when we went upstairs the kids had T'Pau posters on their bedroom walls. On our second viewing I was greeted with a bunch of flowers from the children. We made an offer that was accepted. Then a few days later the estate agent called and said the vendors wanted another five thousand pounds.

Is 5k the price of fame?

When the day came to leave The Pengwern Boat Club, I was so excited. I had loved the place dearly but was ready to move on. Ronnie was really upset. He lay in bed and was very emotional. He had not said anything when we were house hunting and I thought we were on the same page. But he had mixed feelings. Shrewsbury was his home town, all his family were there and although we'd travelled constantly, I didn't realise how much it meant to him. I don't think he did either until the removal van pulled up.

We'd had the best of times and worst of times in Shrewsbury. My story would be incomplete without mentioning Ronnie's beloved mum, Olive, who was such a part of our lives in Shropshire. Olive had been diagnosed with breast cancer while we were recording in America. She was battling bravely but we had to go back to tour. Ronnie called home frequently but she had kept things pretty quiet. On our return from the

States, we went straight home to Shrewsbury to see her and I had to keep the look of horror from my face when we walked into the sitting room.

She hadn't let us know just how ill she was. Olive had always been tall and good-looking with a mass of dark hair. She had beautiful nails and always wore massive blingy rings. She was very glamorous. When we got back, however, she was reed-thin and wearing a wig. It was heart-breaking to see. She was just lying on the sofa and I nearly burst into tears in front of her. Olive was great fun with a sharp sense of humour and we really got on. I loved Olive.   But when we saw her that day, she was quite plainly dying. Ronnie and I went home and were silent. We were in the UK for a while and we were able to see her as often as possible. Then she was taken into the hospital as her condition deteriorated. We were in the studio in London recording a B-side when we got a phone call for Ron. He was told on the phone by his brother that their mum had just passed away.

After the funeral, we went straight back to work and I don't think Ron really had time to grieve for her. Moving away from Shrewsbury seemed to bring all of that into sharp focus.

I was sympathetic to Ronnie and asked him to just give it six months, to see whether things would work out.

As we became successful, our lives changed in many, many ways.

Take money, for instance. When we put in our offer on our house in London, we went to the bank for a mortgage which was based on our projected earnings: things were different then. We were told that the record label, Siren, would advance us the money so there would be no need. We thought that sounded like great news. After all, why pay interest if we didn't need to? What we didn't realise was as the money from Siren was an advance, our manager was able to commission it at 20%. The band were also on a percentage of album sales after costs and that, of course, deferred their profits. Ronnie and I insisted on writing the four guys a cheque for £10,000 each. Our lawyer said we were under no obligation to do this, but we felt terrible. It was the right thing to do. It was naïvely handled on our part and even though Ron and I had the best of intentions, the band were very suspicious and did not appreciate the gesture. I am pretty sure the bank interest on a deposit loan would have been a lot cheaper.

Bridge Of Spies was a hugely successful album and the follow-up, Rage, picked up where BOS left off. Both of them were built on a foundation of solid touring. For a while, it seemed as though we were just away constantly. We were coming home to appear on TV and do other promotional work, but basically we were on the road. I have to admit, I liked it. I had Ronnie with me. We were rock stars with no kids or responsibilities. Funnily enough, I've found a cutting from an interview recently that I did back then which said: 'I'm never having a baby, I'm not the maternal type.' I liked not being accountable to anyone but Ron and myself. I enjoyed just being on the road and doing my thing. Touring is not compatible with family life.

There is a saying on the road: 'What goes on tour stays on tour.' In our case, that was definitely the case. The boys were away from home for a long, long time. Our band was hot and good looking and young girls were throwing themselves at the boys. You know, who knows what I would have done or Ronnie would have done if we'd not been together.

The constant attention from the press began to cause problems, and one area that caused big arguments surrounded the type of media coverage we got. We were picking up features and covers in everything from Smash Hits through to Q, NME and Kerrang!. But as time went on, the coverage became increasingly pop-orientated. Ferret and Spanner, our PR company, were very pop-focused and were getting us to do all the kids' TV shows as well as programmes like Noel's House Party. After showing a fleeting interest in us the 'credible press' turned. Our management and record company were of the opinion that you did everything. They thought there was no such thing as bad publicity.

For my part, I freely admit I had no long-term vision, I didn't look at the bigger picture. I didn't once think: 'Is this the right way for our band to be portrayed?' I never thought about things strategically. I also loved the attention. It made me feel great. But in retrospect, that may not have been the best thing for the band, even though I didn't realise it at the time. T'Pau was always a mix of pop sensibilities and accessibility,

but we were also a really good rock band and Ronnie and I were good
songwriters. We were a contradiction. As the press requests stacked up,
Ron would say: 'No, we should be taken more seriously as musicians.'
He wanted us to be picking and choosing and sometimes saying NO! The
band thought like that as well. Whereas I just thought it was great that
all those journalists wanted to interview me and all those photographers
wanted to take my photo. I genuinely thought it helped to make us
popular.

The band, however, became increasingly fed up of only being on the
cover of teen magazines. They were sick to death of being asked to do
silly poses. They were fast becoming mere background in photographs;
the ancillary personnel to me. Most publications only wanted to talk to
me, too, which also started to cause a problem with the band – and with
Ronnie. He wasn't jealous of the attention I got, but he didn't think it was
the right way to go in terms of our longevity. Maybe he was right.

I really didn't mind doing lifestyle pieces in the supplements or
appearing on silly quiz shows and I still don't. I'm a sociable person and
I can chat about anything. It really didn't bother me. I didn't see what the
problem was. But it was a problem.

Maybe you can't be on the front cover of Smash Hits and Q
Magazine. Maybe you have to decide who you are and pick a side. I
thought that publicity could work on different levels. It really didn't
bother me. But looking back I was too accessible and too eager to
please. If you look at any credible band, they don't smile much, they tell
everyone to f- off, they're often grumpy or late, or off their tits.

I'm quite a straightforward person. I have no guile. I do what I say
I'm going to do when I say I'm going to do it. I smile a lot and I like to
engage people, and I write memorable straightforward MOR pop songs.
If you want to be a credible band, it's not just about the music; you've
also got to be a bit of a cunt and I was too much of a people pleaser. I was
worried it might all disappear if I didn't play ball.

Also if your next record isn't doing so well as the last, everyone starts
to panic and that is contagious. So shit gets thrown at the wall in the hope
that some of it will stick. Based on that wishy-washy, unstrategic attitude

– and my unashamed enjoyment of being famous – I only have myself to blame for a lot of what happened when the credible press began to turn on me. One Melody Maker journalist, David Stubbs, made it his mission to crucify us – and in particular me – every week.

Barbara Ellen, another influential journalist, flew out to interview me and review our show in Switzerland. We were playing a massive gig and she came along with a photographer in tow. We got to work on the photographs and were shooting in a darkened hotel room. Whilst the photographer was taking the shots of me, Barbara was interviewing me in the dark. The photographer was using a very old-fashioned camera with very bleak lighting. He was also using a very slow shutter speed, so I had to keep really still during each shot. He wanted a moody, sleazy picture. He styled me in a bed, with no clothes on. I was wrapped in sheets with Champagne and pizza all over me. The photographer was creating the juxtaposition of junk food, sex and glamour. He wanted to create a piece of art.

I realised straight away that his shots were going to be highly creative, and he and I both threw ourselves into the process.

Barbara, however, continued to interview me at the same time. Except the questions didn't seem like an interview, they felt more like a pub quiz. I found it all a bit sly. I was being asked maths equations, for details of various MPs and for information about former Kings of England. She wanted to know historical dates, too. I did not know some of the answers but I couldn't actually hear her half of the time. But that was beside the point. It was a trap not an interview. When it went to press the whole tone of her feature was: 'She's a bimbo.'

I'd been busy trying to be polite and amenable towards her, not letting her know that inside I was getting embarrassed and pissed off. Instead, I was just trying to please her and go along with it. I knew as we were speaking that it was a hatchet job. It didn't come as a surprise when I read it.

At the concert that evening, my management told me that the journalist was suddenly ill and couldn't make the show. She actually put in the article that she'd managed to fake dysentery to avoid going to the show. I was utterly humiliated.

Hindsight as they say is 20:20. After a plethora of Radio 1 Road Shows and Teddy Bears' picnics, silly articles about how I kept fit and appearances on kiddies TV, by the time we got to our third album, The Promise, we might as well have been Fun Boy Three as far as the credible music press was concerned. I don't mind admitting that I had a chip on my shoulder about it for a long time.

Today I get Tweets and Facebook messages sweetly telling me that T'Pau were one of the most underrated bands that this country every produced, and it breaks my heart every time I read that because it's too late now.

We were very underrated and some of it was of our own doing. In particular, some of it was of my doing because of my ridiculous, puppy-like enthusiasm for everything, as well as my worries, my insecurities and my ego, which constantly needed polishing. Ego isn't necessarily about being arrogant; ego can also be about being quite vulnerable. It's who you are.

I was always keen to please and make it work. I just didn't want to f-up the opportunities that I'd worked so hard for and that I'd strived to get.

So if our PR or record label advised me that something was the right thing to do, even if I felt a bit of a dick doing it, I'd get on and do it. 'The show must go on,' that's what I thought. Though that philosophy only seemed to make Ronnie and the band more and more unhappy.

The wheels, however, were still firmly on the T'Pau juggernaut at that stage. When you achieve that level of success, weird shit starts to happen and something very creepy happened when we had a week of sell-out gigs at Hammersmith Odeon.

We more or less moved in for the week, and I had the first dressing room on the ground floor by the stage. The gigs were going brilliantly and on about day three of the run, I couldn't find my stage clothes. I asked Sally, our wardrobe lady, where my stuff was. She looked in the wardrobe and was at a loss. Our clothes were washed, pressed or dry-cleaned, then delivered back to the dressing room every day. Sally knew where everybody's knickers were. She ran our dressing rooms with remarkable efficiency. But today my stage outfit wasn't there.

In my dressing room, there were three steps up to a small mezzanine area where there was a dressing table. It was where I applied my make-up. If you turned around on that small platform you could see across the top of the wardrobes into the lower half of the room. Sally hunted high and low for my clothes, wondering whether they had been stolen?

We walked up to the top of the mezzanine and as we looked back across the room, we spied a heap of clothing on top of the wardrobes.

Sally was the taller of us and reached up to pull everything down. Sure as anything, the pile comprised my stage clothes. But curiously, they were all stuck together. Sally and I had seen enough crusty sheets in our time to know that somebody had wanked all over them. Some sick bastard had knocked one out all over my Shirley Wong designer outfit. Maybe it was more than one guy as there was a lot of … well you know where I'm going with this. Was it a 'phwoar' or a 'take that, bitch?' I know it shouldn't matter. But I felt like it was a horrible act of defilement. In truth, it was all a bit scary. We had high security by then. So the finger of suspicion pointed at the people who'd got 'access all areas' passes. I guess I'll never know.

T'Pau had some great fans and the relationship between band and audience was good. Of course, you'd get the odd nutter, too, and I had some strange fan mail as well as some very pornographic fan mail. One particularly worrying letter came from an HM Prison.

Prisoners' letters have to be read before they are sent and the person who had read that one had gone through it with a big black marker pen. Most of it was crossed out. It was just lots of black marker. It went along the lines of: 'What I really love is ...' and ' Before lights out I like to...' followed by a big line of black Sharpie cross outs. Not a lot of the letter was left so I don't know what that gentleman had to say to me.

I had another letter from a guy in the UAE. The letter started out very nice and the writer was knowledgeable about our music. He told me which were his favourite songs, complimented me on my voice, and then it descended into graphic sexual detail. He wished I had been in the scene in Basic Instinct uncrossing my legs with no panties on, and finished by asking me to post a small clipping of pubes to him. I laughed a lot of it off because I've always been one of the lads and I'm not going to get up in arms at stupid male behaviour. We just threw it away. If it was anything scary I might have worried, but there wasn't anything that frightened me.

They were just silly tossers – and, at The Hammersmith Odeon, I meant that quite literally.

The prize for the nastiest fan mail came after I'd said in an article that Wellington, where I grew up, was a dull, boring little town. I got a few letters saying: 'Don't show your face back here, you f-ing snotty bitch.'

I appreciate normal people who don't gush, who aren't sycophantic and aren't overwhelmed and tongue-tied. I like the people who treat me normally and who have the confidence to just be cool. They come up and say: 'I love your music,' or 'I like the lyrics in that song.' They talk knowledgeably about the music, and tell me stories about how a song of ours got them through their exams, or that China was the first tune that was played at their wedding. They tell me that our songs mean a lot to them. It is a great honour to have been part of the soundtrack to some people's lives. That is a huge compliment. As an angst-driven teenager, I hung on every lyric of certain songs too, so I understand exactly how they feel.

I also really appreciate a lively audience. I give the same level of performance whether I'm in an arena, a club or a theatre-sized venue, and I like a good response for my efforts.

When you play a theatre venue, you have all the production bells and whistles including 'follow spotlights'. Those are the big lights operated from 'the gods' by follow-spot operators, so that key performers are illuminated at all times. The lead singer will usually be in the follow spot all the time and they blind you. Imagine someone shining a gigantic torch in your eyes, that'll give you an idea of what it's like. You can't see much outside of that arc of light, just vague shadows, and it's almost like playing to a vast, empty black space. When I talk to a theatre audience, I often put my hand up to block the follow spot so I can see people's faces, a bit like blocking out the sun.

On one occasion, we were playing a large theatre in Leeds. I could see shadows outside of the light and people were really dancing in the aisles and getting down at the back of the theatre. Theatres can often be intimidating to an audience and they feel self-conscious about standing up and letting themselves go, especially if they're at the front. On that particular night, we were totally rocking out and I was pissed off with all the seated stick-in-the-muds at the front. I wanted the crazy people from the back to come forward. So I said: 'Why don't you lot swap places and let those people who are really enjoying themselves come down to the front? I want that energy!'

What I didn't realise was that the people at the front were all in wheelchairs and I couldn't see them. The band were mouthing 'noooooo' at me. Some of them did try to get up after I said that.

After we finished touring Rage we were exhausted. We had not stopped for two years. We were tired and we'd run out of songs. At one point, BOS was in the bottom reaches of the top 100 albums as Rage was in the top 10. Again with the brilliance of hindsight, it's easy to conclude that we released Rage too soon. We should have taken a gap when we were big enough to be able to do that.

Rage achieved impressive Platinum sales. But it was not quadruple Platinum, as BOS had been. Our impact was lessening because we were over-saturating the market. Secret Garden, the first single, peaked at number 18, the beautiful ballad Road To Our Dream stalled at 44 – shocking for me, as I really love that song. Only The Lonely did slightly better at 28, but there was no number one; there wasn't even a top 10.

The videos for all three songs had been directed, as always, by Brian Grant and they were stunning big budget, mini movies. We all consoled ourselves that the album had still done well, going Platinum, and all artists have their peaks and troughs. By now, however, it was time to get writing and produce a third album.

There were other issues for Ronnie and I to deal with. We were getting more and more frustrated by the apparent lack of strategy that our manager, Chris, had for us. He was being kept very busy with his new client, Curiosity Killed the Cat. They were beautiful young fashionable boys, media darlings: looking back they were forerunners for the Made In Chelsea set.

They were shooting a video with Andy Warhol, hanging out in the hippest clubs and dating lanky models. We were a clonky old '80s pop-rock band and we were already becoming seen as yesterday's news.

Faced with a dip in our popularity, we very much needed some focused, clever management.

Chris came up with the idea of a one-off show called 'One Night With T'Pau' at The Caird Hall in Dundee. Whilst we were busy writing, the show was to be our only gig of the year. It was to be an exciting one-off event to give our profile a little bounce in autumn 1989. Sorry Dundee, no offence. But was that really the best he could come up with? A provincial Scottish town was our big one-off show for the year? The location didn't make sense.

It turned out he knew a local promoter up there who was a mate. We arrived the day before the show to set up the production, with a tour bus and an artic' full of gear. As we rolled into town, we could not see any posters on our route in so we detoured all round the city to check. It was the same elsewhere: there was not one. We then learned that ticket sales were not good. The show was only about a third sold.

I was furious and got on the phone to Chris. He told us to, and I quote: 'Drive the tour bus through the town to cause a buzz.' We then had to have garish Day-Glo Quad Cap posters quickly made and get someone to distribute them around the town, desperately trying to generate some publicity in the last 24 hours. We were physically promoting our own show. It was beyond embarrassing.

We did the show and the last-minute walk-up was OK. But the venue was not full and had not been properly promoted. Chris was nowhere to be seen. Then Teresa, our PA, left. She was deeply unhappy with several things, and the world dropped out of our management team. Financial issues raised their ugly head and almost instantly it was over.

The schism made Ronnie and me really sad. We'd had a lot of laughs and Chris had been quite a father figure to us. The ride we'd been on together had been so exciting, but inevitably things changed. A complicated legal process began and it took the best part of four years to resolve. Ronnie and I were quickly snapped up by Chris O'Donnell and Chris Morrison of Morrison/O'Donnell (clearly you have to be called Chris to be a manager). They were looking after Blur and The Beloved, so we thought: 'Yeah! We've got cool managers now, things will pick up!' They oversaw our third album for Siren/Virgin, The Promise.

By now, the band wanted more creative input, and Ronnie and I were happy to write with them as they were good musicians and quite frankly, we didn't have the time to write a whole album on our own. We booked into a few residential studios dotted around the countryside and holed ourselves up to write. Residential studios are like hotels. You eat, work and sleep there. Ronnie and I had also been writing at home and had about six songs ready. The collective songs were written either by all six of us, or three or four of us. As the lyricist, I was entitled under publishing rules to claim half the song. I have never done that, however, as I think when a group of people write a song together, one hand washes the other. You feed off each other's ideas – I lived to regret the decision.

See You Around

By the time of the third album, things between the band and us were not as good as they had been. Ronnie and I had, by now, begun to earn pretty good money from the royalties earned by BOS and Rage. The band were on handsome, monthly retainers, a percentage of tour merchandise and record sales, but Ronnie and I wrote all the songs so all the publishing was ours. Money from the record sales was a moot point as the label recouped first and divided any profits later. I am still to this day un-recouped on sales, so the band would not have had that money either.

It began to cause resentment that our incomes differed so much. I covered earlier the mistake we made in buying our house with an advance from Siren. Suddenly Ron and I were in a different league financially. But as I saw it, the boys were on a great deal as jobbing musicians. I think where the problem came was that we were sold as a band, and acted like a band, but only Ronnie and I were signed to the label, and we wrote all the songs.

They genuinely felt that they helped to create the success of T'Pau and to an extent they did. Our A&R guy Simon Hicks once told me that in America, Michael had bent his ear one night at a bar, saying nobody gave a fuck who played keyboards in T'Pau. Simon bluntly replied: 'You're right, but Carol and Ronnie do give a fuck, so you'd be wise to appreciate that.' It's not something I ever wanted to give breath to; I did not want to be forced to say it to them out loud. I really loved our band, we were by now close friends, but many good musicians could have been in that line-up. By the time we found Dean, he was our third guitarist, Paul was our second bass player. Michael wouldn't even join the band until we could guarantee him money. Neither he, nor Dean, were in the band when we got our deal. Die-hard fans love an original line-up I know, but being brutal, the core of T'Pau was Ron and I as writers, then I was the front person and face of the band. And for me on purely an emotional level, Tim Burgess our drummer was part of the heart of the band. After Chris introduced us, the three of us had been inseparable. Being on the opposing side to Tim was tough.

But my loyalty to the band was being tested. Morrison/O'Donnell, who did not think they had the right to renegotiate their deal with us, wanted us to fire them. They saw them simply as players on a good wage. But Ronnie and I were loyal, and we wanted to keep the band together. We'd all been so happy together in the beginning. We were like family. We'd also been through enough changes and problems with our first manager, and couldn't bear the thought of anything else going wrong, so Ronnie and I decided to negotiate. Looking back now, it would have been so much easier to serve them notice as we were entitled to. We could have got session guys in and saved ourselves a lot of unnecessary pain.

Negotiations were not easy or conveniently timed. We were now in Rockfield Studios in Monmouth, recording The Promise with producer

Andy Richards. Andy, like Gary Langan, was an ex-Trevor Horn cohort. He had a different way of producing. He used a Fairlight digital sampling keyboard. He would programme what we played into it and quantize drums and riffs, and even backing vocals, so they played back in precise time. That produced a more precise-sounding record. Some would argue it was clinical. We wanted a new sound though and it was considered a very modern way of recording.

Whilst we were trying to make the record, we were also all constantly on the phone to our various lawyers. The control room phone would ring, the studio receptionist would say: 'It's the band's lawyer on the phone.' They would leave the control room for 20 minutes, then come back in silently. Then the phone would ring again and it would be our lawyer, so Ronnie and I would step out and hear what their lawyer had proposed. But we never spoke to each other. It was like a bad divorce. Only the lawyers win. The final straw came when, in order to get what they wanted, they withdrew permission for six of the songs they had co-written to be used on the album, even though we were in the middle of recording it. They out-voted Ronnie and I by four against two on those co-writes. That is when I regretted not taking 50% for the lyrics.

They had us over a barrel. We were completely out-manoeuvred and so far down the line with the album that we had to suck it up. But that was the beginning of the end. I was livid!

And as I saw it, we'd just been blackmailed.

The atmosphere in the studio was fraught: poor Andy, he must have regretted working with us. As if that wasn't enough, I also suffered the painful loss of my father while we were recording. He suffered a massive heart attack at home in Nuneaton. He was only 57.

My father had been one of the great pillars of my life. He was a brilliant pianist. He had all his certificate distinctions by the age of 12 and 13, which I still have on my wall. He was a lover of jazz piano, he was a really talented guy. He played in all the clubs in Liverpool when he was young.

I had, as I mentioned before, received financial and emotional support from both my parents. The only time Dad ever expressed a tad of concern was when I was 27. He said: 'You're 30 in three years, have you thought about doing the cruises? You'll still be singing and at least you'll be starting to earn some money.' But that to me was the equivalent of a musical day job. I was horrified. But that made sense to my Dad. He wanted me to still do what I loved, but to find a way of making a living. He wanted me to survive.

Dad had osteoarthritis and had just had one knee replacement. We were all very focused on his knees, we had no idea he had heart problems too.

When he died, we found out from a neighbour that they'd had a pint in the local and Dad had said that he'd had really weird pains down his left arm. Dad's friend had made him promise he would go to the doctors for a check-up and he had apparently done so. During the wake at Mum's house, the doctor phoned up saying they'd like to see Dad. They had the results of his blood test and were concerned. It was too little, too late.

Dad died on December 19th, 1990, on the kitchen floor, in my Mum's arms. My brother had to fight tooth and nail with the crematorium to get him cremated before the Christmas holidays started as they closed for two weeks. He wanted some closure before Christmas. They were not co-operative, so we had to move heaven and earth to get them to agree.

Mum went into shock and did not speak or cry for about four days.

Dad was to be cremated at 5pm on Christmas Eve. It was, of course, very dark at that time of year at 5pm. Waiting for the hearse to arrive at the house with Dad, I stood at the end of the drive looking out for him. As the hearse rounded the corner I shouted back to the house: 'He's here!' Every single light in the house went out. All the fuses blew. I am sad to say that no one in the band sent my Mum a card or flowers.

With Andy Richards producing The Promise, we hoped we were moving forward. We'd done our first two albums with Roy, and all of our videos with Brian Grant. We had this formula going, which had certainly worked well for a while. But now it was time for change. The political climate was in upheaval then. Margaret Thatcher was on her last legs in Number 10.

The knives were out for her from her former closest allies, and after

11 years of her being Prime Minister, it was hard to imagine her not being in the top job, beating up usurpers with her handbag. In our downtime, we were all glued to the news. Would she stay or would she go? Andy Richards said: 'Not a chance.' We all said: 'We think this is it.'

A late night, beer-fuelled political debate ensued. Andy said he was so confident that the Iron Lady would never resign, he would shave off his moustache if she did. He'd had a moustache his entire adult life. His son had never seen him without it. In fact, Andy had such a big Freddie Mercury yard brush under his nose, I assumed he was gay.

When Maggie fell on her sword in November 1990, we presented Andy with a fresh Bic razor and sent him off to the bathroom. He emerged sans 'tache and was actually shaking – and a bit tearful – as it had been such a drastic step for him to take. He wasn't sure how he'd look. On a trip home to London when we took a few days off, his son freaked out as the strange man tried to hug him. His face has been as smooth as a baby's bum ever since. We did him a favour!

The Promise was released in June 1991. In the years since Rage had been released in 1988, the world had changed. The overblown excesses and glamour of the '80s were reviled and replaced by Grunge and Indie.

Kate Moss was the new cover girl. American bands like Nirvana, Pearl Jam, The Smashing Pumpkins and Soundgarden were taking over from the likes of Bon Jovi and Van Halen. Back home The Stone Roses, Radiohead, The Charlatans, Oasis and Blur were on their way to becoming the new Indie Kings. I loved all those bands, but I could never emulate them and would have looked ridiculous trying to. We were in a new era where the pop artists ruling the roost were Back Street Boys, N'Sync, Take That and – soon after – The Spice Girls.

Our erstwhile brand of pop rock did not fit in anywhere. The album scraped into the top 10 and achieved Gold status, but the singles, Whenever You Need Me Need and Walk On Air made little impact. It was gutting. I felt bad for Andy Richards as the album sounded – and still sounds – beautiful.

The Promise is cruelly underrated. The songs are well-written, catchy and melodic, well-played and well-sung. The album is well-produced.

But the public was not buying it. Andy had produced a good album for an imploding band. We were committed to a European and UK tour. But there was nothing planned in the rest of the world. Our appeal was vastly diminished. In the wake of The New Order, we were dead in the water.

Not long after that time a friend of mine, Gràinne Fletcher, who also worked on our PR, owned a restaurant in St John's Wood with her husband, Andy Fletcher from Depeche Mode. I used to hang out there. One evening I was at the bar, Liam Gallagher was also there and he was at the height of his fame. He was a bit pissed and said to me: 'Eh Carol, the '80s were yours, but it's all over now eh? This is our time.' There's nothing like rubbing your nose in it.

I nicknamed The Promise Tour, The Walkman Tour. Now on the tour bus we were not gossiping and laughing round the tables, or playing cards and watching videos together, but all staring glumly out of respective windows with our headphones on.

We had brought in two girls for the tour, Linda Duggan on backing vocals and Bernita on saxophone. It was a breath of fresh air having some new personnel, and a real treat to have the sax break on China as-per-the record instead of on a guitar. The girls were great; Linda in particular was a party animal. She would go off to clubs with the band or crew after shows, party like a lunatic, have about three hours sleep and still sing like a demon the next day; that was her routine. She had the hardcore Irish drinking gene. I was so envious as I lose my voice if I do that. I have spent 30 years worrying about catching a cold or staying up too late.

Plus, although I am an enthusiastic drinker, I have always been rubbish at it, suffering horrendous hangovers. Teresa always teased me that I was 'born to be mild'.

The popular recreational drug at that time was E. It made some of us temporarily love each other for a few hours after show time. However, although we did good shows and did have some laughs along the way, things were not the same.

Before long, Linda and Bernita were privy to what was going on. A couple of the band were unable to keep their own counsel, particularly after a few drinks, and had bent the girls' ears about recent events. The atmosphere was like being back at my bitchy, catty, girls' school. If I walked into a room, it fell silent. I was sharing a dressing room with Linda, and I got upset one day as I felt so alienated from everyone else. I could see the end was coming. Linda eventually told me that I was not popular with the band anymore, and was very much seen as the resident evil. Ronnie seemed free of any criticism. He was one of the lads. I was a bitch, of course. The whole scenario created an enormous strain on me. I'd have to bite my tongue so we could go on stage every night and give a good show. Keeping up your Hollywood face can be exhausting at the best of times – but it's hell when you're dying inside.

The venues were smaller again. We had moved back down from arenas to the theatres like Hammersmith Odeon and Manchester Apollo, where on previous tours we had been given the house award for selling out five shows in a row, twice. This time we struggled to fill two nights.

After we came off stage at the Hammersmith Odeon one night, my manager Chris O'Donnell came into my dressing room. I was still dripping with sweat and catching my breath. Instead of congratulating me on a good show, his opening words were: 'You are a very lucky girl – you just walked away from an £800,000 debt.'

Knowing that despite our success we were still un-recouped at Virgin, I said: 'The label just dropped us, didn't they?' Chris said: 'It's an opportunity.'

I didn't see it that way at all. To be dropped mid-tour was humiliating. That information would shoot around the industry like wild fire. We now had to do the European leg of the tour, performing a record no-one was interested in. We were in a band that was falling apart, and we had no record label to support us with our PR and media. We were on our own.

We let the band know on the tour, but the rest of the tour was a low-key, depressing affair.

I remember the year before we had played a large festival in Europe with Jethro Tull, and they all turned up in separate limos. We were astonished as their cavalcade of cars streamed past us in the artist enclosure. We learned that it was because they couldn't stand each other anymore so they travelled separately. The only time they were willing to be together was when they were on stage. We'd turned into that band. Everything had turned sour. We went from being great pals, from feeling we were in safe hands with Chris and with a big label behind us, then all of a sudden we had nothing. Everything we'd worked for and built together was just blown away. It went almost as quickly as it came.

By this time, I had also had it with being blatantly snubbed and blamed for everything. When we landed at Heathrow after the last show, we collected our luggage and came through customs, looking for our drivers. I turned to face the guys and said: 'See you around.'

As soon as we got home we made arrangements for their one-month notice to be served. The letters were sent out. It was a curt and formal ending to our six years together.

I have not seen Michael or Paul since that day. Michael and I have had no contact at all. I am happy to say that Dean, Tim and I made our peace years later. Paul and I have exchanged emails now and again. Tim and I talk regularly; in fact, he's helped me a lot trying to recall events for this book in the right order, something we both found challenging.

Both the boys and I could have handled things better. I was by no means blameless. I was affronted and very hurt at the low opinion they had of me because I disagreed with them, and yet they had no problem with Ronnie, who is very much his own man and was party to all the decisions. But I wish that I'd had the maturity to keep my ego out of it. To this day, if I have to reflect, like now, on how things ended, I still feel so sad that something so special ended in bitter disarray.

Carol and Ronnie together on stage again

Above - And my friends told me I was born to be mild . . .

Below - Loved my Mum. Always there for a chat and a fag.

Top: With Bill Wyman

Left: I was always destined to perform. I identified with fashion, music and drama from an early age.

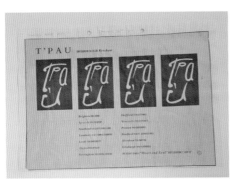

Above - The Hammy Odeon became a home-from-home as we sold out a week-long residency

Left, top - The Nik Kershaw tour helped us to build our audience. I went back on the road with Nik in 2015.

Left, bottom - We missed out on a BRIT - but won the Northallerton Public Opinion Certificate. Back of the net!

Top: My secret garden. Life on the road.

Left - Being stopped for selfies with fans had become our life by the late 1980s

Top and left - The arrival of Scarlett framed the happy domestic life that Richard and I led

Below - Becoming a mum was a far cry from the era of gigs at London's legendary Marquee Club

SANDRINGHAM HOUSE

Dear Miss Decker,

    I just wanted to write and say how touched I was
that you felt able to take part in the recent Prince's
Trust Gala at the London Palladium. It was extremely
generous of you and I can't tell you how much I
appreciated such a kind gesture. Apart from anything
else I <u>really</u> enjoyed the contribution you made on
stage, and I thought the whole evening was a stunning,
professional success.

    As a result of your participation we will be able
to help many more young people achieve their potential,
and that is what really matters.

    This brings you my warmest thanks and best wishes.

Yours sincerely

Charles

Top: I still love to get
my rocks off on the
big stages. Inset -
with Peter Hook and
Eddi Reader

Left: A letter from
Prince Charles

When I re-emerged with new songs and a new image I had to decide
whether to work as Carol Decker, or continue as T'Pau

I've rarely worked so much as in recent years. Festivals were made for T'Pau.
Dylan and Scarlett got in on the act at Rewind

A wall full of highs and lows from my life. No names, no packdrill - to protect the innocent . . . and the guilty.

Above - Rockin' it

Left - Laminates from our tours around the globe remind us of where we've been

Above - Take your kids to your wedding - it's the only way. With Richard, Dylan and Scarlett on our Big Day

Left - Toasting the nuptials. We all ended up in the pool

Below - The Brits party was a night of excess

Back where it all began, in Shrewsbury

My family are my life. With Richard, Dylan and Scarlett.

Forever on the road. I was born to entertain.

Murphy And The Steak Fat

After The Promise Tour finished and we no longer had a record deal, Ronnie and I spent more time at our place in Monmouth. We had bought a large house with some land and installed a big studio with a live room. We didn't really know what to do other than keep writing. We invited lots of our music pals down to stay and we'd have writing weekends. We had a sort of collective going including Scotty, who'd helped us that day to get our deal; Alan Thomson, Aran Ahmun and Spencer Cozens from the Julia Fordham band. We'd met all those guys through Taj, whom we had stayed pals with. They were a 'jazzier' bunch and brought a different feel to the writing. Morrison/O'Donnell did not seem to be making progress on getting interest from labels, so we asked to be released from our management contract with them. Chris Morrison went ape-shit on the phone. But in my view, things hadn't moved on. Chris O'Donnell on the other hand was perfectly reasonable. He saw it wasn't working for them or for us, and he calmed Morrison down. Chris Morrison had by that time had two heart by-pass operations. O'Donnell used to gag he was such a ruthless manager, he'd had it done on purpose.

We had spent some time out in LA writing. Virgin Music had put us together with Richard Feldman, a successful writer who had written for Belinda Carlisle. One of the tracks, Make Love To Me, had come out really well. Along our travels and due to a loose association with Queen, via RTB, I had met Jim Beach, their manager. I got chatting to him at a showbiz bash and he'd asked to hear some songs so we sent over a few.

He really liked MLTM, but thought it needed a production overhaul. He also thought I should now be a solo artist. Ronnie was fine with that, in fact, he was relieved. I was becoming hard to live with, as I was stressing out about getting going again and recovering my poll position in the charts and in the music business. I was depressed and desperate.

Ronnie had by now tired of a lot of the bullshit associated with trying to keep a band going, and he was sick of the business in general. He was also coming to his wits' end trying to keep me happy, and was more than happy to be my writing partner, helping me on my way with Jim Beach, just as he had with Lulu and The UK Players.

Jim booked me into The Strongroom Studios and put a production team around me. We did a hi-nrg pop version of MLTM, which was going to be my first solo single.

It was quite a departure and really veering toward a really light programmed pop thing. At the time I really liked it, but then I always love everything when I am recording. I get caught up in the creation process. I enjoy the company of good musicians and egghead engineers admiring how clever they all are. It often takes a week or so for me to calm down, and then listen objectively and analyse whether or not it's actually any good. I took the finished product home to Ronnie and he absolutely hated it. In fact, he thought I had lost my mind

He said: 'Are you serious? You're much better than that.' He thought it was like throwaway Stock Aitken Waterman stuff. And that completely gutted me because I needed to believe in it. I was desperate for the project to work. I had Jim Beach in my corner, one of the biggest managers in the world. Ron said: 'Don't do this, you'll bury yourself, it's completely the wrong thing for you, it's the wrong way to go.' After a day or so listening to the track, I realised Ronnie was right, it was awful.

I complied a lengthy fax to Jim expressing my gratitude, but saying I had decided on reflection that the style was not right. I asked if we could try it more our way? Could we try a couple of songs with his guys but direct it more?

I got no reply. I called Jim in Switzerland. His PA said: 'I'm so sorry Carol, but that's the way he is. He felt this was a good first step for you. If you don't want to take his advice, it's over.' I never heard from Jim again. I'll never know what might have been.

Eventually our version of MLTM was included on my album Red.

Ronnie thought it was time I went off and did my own thing, and I also think Ronnie needed the space. But I didn't know who I was going to be if I wasn't this person I'd always aspired to be. I'd actually invented myself, I'd invented this successful rock star. If I wasn't that person then who was I? My identity disappeared when T'Pau dissolved.

We had two houses and we had 10 acres of land down in Wales, and a big studio. We were doing okay financially but not emotionally. Ronnie also started to feel down. He had lost a lot as well, especially his mum. We had been so busy that he had not really had time to process her death. They were very close. On top of that, it was the end of T'Pau, and he also had to deal with a manic depressive girlfriend running around like a chicken with its head cut off while trying to be famous again.

We were both not in a great place. Everything had gone from brilliant to awful. Ronnie can be quiet and reflective as a person, but he was getting quieter and quieter, and I started having recurrent anxiety dreams that he didn't love me anymore. I'd wake up and I would be in a hot sweat. My subconscious knew something was wrong.

We would always tell each other, regularly, that we loved each other. We were very physical, very tactile and affectionate. Lately, I noticed that if I took him up a cup of tea to the studio and tried to cuddle him, he'd take the tea and give me a little peck, but he'd gently ease me away. I thought he was just really focused and preoccupied, as was normal while he was in the studio. I even gave him a silly nickname 'Mr Kissy-Away.' I would playfully chastise him that he was always too busy for a kiss, and would literally 'kiss me away.'

He needed time on his own to figure out how he felt about everything, including me, but did not know how to tell me. Anyway, he was feeling so rubbish that I suggested he see a counsellor, not expecting that he'd agree as blokes can often be too proud to do stuff like that. To my surprise he did.

Whenever he came back from a session, I would enquire if he felt it had gone okay and helped him, though I tried not to pry. I too was feeling empty. I was getting bored in Monmouth and now Ronnie never wanted to be in London. I felt buried alive down there. The halcyon days of the

South Wales Massive were long gone. People had moved on. We were
now just living in a small Welsh town. We were no longer recording
in Rockfield and partying with Robert Plant. It was just a regular,
monotonous daily life. We limped on for the next year, a pale shadow of
the loving couple we had been.

Finally came the day I will never forget: it was Valentine's Day 1993
and it was a Sunday morning. I'd gone downstairs and got all the papers.
We had tea and toast and I took that back up to our room. I was flicking
through all the Valentine's stuff in the supplements.

I turned to Ronnie and said: 'Do you know, I can't remember the last
time you told me that you loved me.' And he said, after a pause: 'Maybe
that's because I'm not sure if I do anymore.'

I nearly threw up. I felt like I had been kicked in the stomach. Tears
filled my eyes, I could barely breathe but managed to utter: 'You don't
love me anymore?' He said: 'I don't know.' Realisation dawned on me
that for quite a while now Ronnie had been saying 'thank you' whenever
I said that I loved him. He then told me his counsellor had suggested he
was in a stagnant relationship, and advised him to say thank you when I
expressed my love as Ronnie didn't feel he could say it back anymore but
didn't want to hurt me.

I said: 'How long have you been feeling like this?' He said: 'About
a year.' A year! He'd been unhappy with me for a year. I had not seen it,
but at the same time somehow knew it. I recovered my composure as best
I could, but I felt like my heart had been ripped from my chest. I just got
in my car and went to the London house. I cried so much on the way I
could barely see the road. Ronnie stayed in Monmouth.

I phoned my best mate, Jennie, who was now living in LA. I sobbed
down the phone: 'Ronnie said he doesn't know if he loves me anymore.'
And characteristically straightforward Jennie said: 'Well then you tell
Ronnie to fuck off until he's made his mind up.' So I just jumped on a
plane and went to stay with her in LA for a few months.

Jennie had by now married Jerry Napier, the sound engineer on
BOS. To my horror, they had started to see each other as our recording
progressed and had kept up a long distance relationship that I hoped

would fizzle out. He was a difficult, grumpy and critical guy. When T'Pau was over, Jennie did not want to tour manage, as a career. For her, it was all about being in our little touring family. She didn't know what to do about their relationship either because she really liked him. Against my better judgement, I told her she should go and see if it was the real deal. I didn't like him, but I had to be a good friend.

So that was tricky, as Jerry and I had to try and be civil as we both loved Jen, and I was living in their house. I settled into a routine of doing some writing out there again, shopping, drinking a lot of cocktails and generally trying to get my head together.

Their house was out in Tajunga, beautifully set amongst the prehistoric-looking California Hills, which rose above the house. Jennie and I would spend a lot of time in their outdoor hot tub, with the stars twinkling above us. We did a lot of drinking and I did a lot of crying. Jennie would come home from work and ask Jerry how I was, and I would hear him sigh and say: 'She's crying . . . again!'

I phoned Ronnie regularly but he never ever phoned me. I would always ask him if he loved me and he would always reply: 'I don't know.'

After about three months I thought: 'I should go home and see what the future holds.' Initially I fooled myself into thinking that I could live with it. He wasn't saying he didn't love me, which meant he could possibly love me again soon.

But it was not to be. I was lonely in my own relationship. I must have cut a pathetic figure hanging on, but I had loved him so much and for so long, I could not accept it was over. One day I was in Monmouth and I got a call to perform on a Welsh TV show called What's That Noise. Ronnie and I had been commissioned by the late film director Michael Winner to rework a very old song from 1864 by Stephen Foster, called Beautiful Dreamer, for his new film Dirty Weekend. This was a promotional opportunity to showcase the track.

I had to stay over on location with the TV crew and band. To cut a long story short, I got drunk and bonked the drummer. Up until that point there had been no one else involved in our relationship problems. And then, that night, I felt wanted for the first time in a long time. I broke the bond with infidelity. I knew it was safe to assume that if Ronnie and I ever broke up, it would probably be impossible for the band to carry on but I had not expected that the end of the band would be the end of us. I didn't know that the band's momentum was also the momentum of our relationship. I never told Ronnie about it until long after we separated.

I felt ashamed. I also felt I had to justify what I had done, so I convinced myself I had real feelings for the drummer hereafter known as Rebound Man (RM). Rebound Man then left for New York, where he had a girlfriend and was in the throws of emigrating when he and I had our fateful evening. I was now in double trouble. I had left Ronnie, left Monmouth, but RM had left too, and I had not been alone since I was 22.

I was now 36. I did not know how to be on my own. I would go to the pub on my own and get plastered, stagger home and call Ronnie at two or three in the morning sobbing. That went on for months. I frequently called Simon and his wife, and sobbed all over them. Simon, Ronnie and I had been like the three musketeers at one point.

Ronnie and I had to meet up in London to sort out our financial and property situation. It was painful but very straightforward. We did not need lawyers. Our accountant sorted it all out. We split all our money 50/50 and kept a house each. I stayed in London. Ronnie kept Monmouth. We were now officially separated.

Then I got a call out of the blue from RM. He said he couldn't stop thinking about me and was thinking of coming back. After being initially frosty as I had not heard from him for months, I was won over by his interest in me as I felt romance was in the air, and he took my mind off my loss. I persuaded him – and myself – that we were in love, and suggested he come back to London and move in with me.

The day I met him at the airport with his trolley piled to the rafters with cases – he had emigrated – my heart sank as I knew I had made a terrible mistake. He probably felt the same. It was a decision made out of fear and desperation. That had been my standard MO for some time.

The relationship was awful, and it didn't take long to discover that RM was a gigolo. Things had not worked out in New York. He was an unsuccessful musician, now in his forties, and was the oldest courier in town. He was not making headway in the music scene as fast as he'd hoped, and I could quickly see he thought I would be good for his career. Mistake. I was no longer even good for my own. He was a stoner, on the weed every night. I hated how it made him even more useless than he normally was. I was drinking a lot as I was so unhappy. He didn't drink so he would criticise me for that, and we would have furious rows.

He was controlling. I was used to an easy-going man in Ronnie, and nobody had told me what to do since I was a young child. He was a psychological bully. He would tell me I should watch my step with him as I was pushing 40, and no one would want me if I lost him. He told me he hated how my stomach bloated just before my period, he said it was disgusting. He made me feel washed-up and ugly. He never took me out and if we did go somewhere, I was the one who paid. He drove my MX5 everywhere and never put petrol in it.

Once my whole family were down and I took them to a fancy restaurant in Notting Hill. My mother was horrified as he ordered two starters!

My family was very concerned that he had got his hooks into me. My cousin Paul, a 6ft 4 inch ex-sailor, even offered to come and change the locks.

We had a volatile relationship. He never laid a hand on me, but would intimidate me by getting right in my face when we argued. He would stay inches from my nose, moving in sync with me as I tried to escape. One day, pushed past my limits with his criticising, I threw a shoe at him and split his bottom lip open. It felt great!

During those awful years, at my worst times, I would drink myself into the floor most nights. I would drink two bottles of wine a night. I started taking drugs too. I'd never been a drug user but I took my first line of coke at the age of 38.

I started going to parties and thinking: 'Does it really matter anymore?' I got to a stage where I felt I didn't really need to preserve my voice any longer or look after myself. Nobody else was interested, so I didn't see why I should be. Nobody gave a shit, so I started doing all sorts of weird things. I had such low esteem. I didn't treat myself with any respect. And although I would never ever have committed suicide, I often didn't care whether I woke up again. I used to wake up on the floor. I woke up in my own vomit more times than I care to remember. I was not in a good place. I was hurting. I couldn't see any reason to carry on.

The drink and coke would numb the pain but when I came back down, I went lower and lower. I'd go further down than I'd been before. And alcohol is a depressant as well. So for that temporary oblivion, I paid a much higher price the next day. The only thing that helped me crawl back out of it was another drink. I felt very bad.

I put myself through that torment for three years. I had no sense of myself anymore and almost no recollection of what I had achieved.

I found out from a mutual friend that Ronnie now had a girlfriend, and that hit me really hard as I knew he had stayed single for quite a while, despite there being an obvious queue for my side of the bed when I left. To think of him with someone else broke my heart. The fact he had taken some time to be alone, before dating again highlighted what a mess I was making of my life.

RM and I realised we could not go on as we were. A friend of his was tour managing Kylie and wanted someone to flat-sit as he was away for months. It was a perfect opportunity to get him out of my house. We still attempted some sort of relationship, but it was more about having someone to escort me if I went out. Also by now, after three bloody years of him, I had made friends with some of his crowd. They included a lot of nice musicians who had no idea what he was like to me in private. I didn't want to lose the few pals I now had in my sad little life. But at last I had some distance from him.

By now, it was 1997 and our local pub, The Lord Palmerston, had been taken over by a chap called Simon Palmer. Simon ran The Lansdowne, in trendy Primrose Hill, one of the hippest places in London. My manor, Tufnell Park and Kentish Town, were not considered to be hip at all. It was a scruffy part of London, full of hideous old boozers that stank of fags, sold warm beer, bad wine and stale cheese and onion baps. Simon was on the crest of the Gastro Pub wave, however. He had a reputation for being a bit of a Basil Fawlty landlord, but he ran a cool bar with excellent food.

I felt a bit sorry for some of my older, more traditional neighbours, in particular John the Cabbie. He liked a pint and a ciggie after work. He said: 'Carol I don't want to smell garlic cooking as I have my pint.' But I loved it as all the trendy Primrose Hillbillies started coming to the end of my road. It was quite exciting. Well-known actors and musicians, cool media types and other funky people started to litter the place. Suddenly, I didn't have to travel for an interesting night out and some decent food.

The Gastro Pub was a different kind of pub. It was more like a Bistro, so I could also prop up the bar without feeling conspicuous as a single woman. I could order a meal and get chatting to someone. A good pub is like a church, with all walks of life there. The bar is the altar.

Working behind the bar was an actor called George. Like all good bar tenders, he was a font of knowledge and a bit of a confidant. He knew who I was, and he knew things were not going too well. One day he pointed out a rather large chap in a chair, tucking into a big old steak. He had a big black coat on. He looked like Orson Welles in the Sandeman port advert. George said: 'You should talk to that guy over there, he's got his own record company in Primrose Hill.' I'd had a few glasses of wine; I looked over and I could see the guy was looking at me. I could tell he knew who I was. And so I went over, buoyed by the wine, and cheekily said: 'So, you've got your own record company?' He replied: 'No, actually, I have a video production company.' I laughed and said: 'So you're of no use to me whatsoever, then.' And he said: 'I don't know, I might be.'

So I pulled up a chair and started having this brilliantly funny conversation with Will Ashurst. He was witty, funny, and as cheeky and irreverent as I am. We hit it off straight away.

Will had worked for EMI for years, in their legal department. He knew all about the music business and was pretty cynical about it. He now had his own video production company called Telegram. He was doing pretty well too. He knew loads of people. He was entrepreneurial and liked to think outside the box – something I have never been any good at and always admire in others.

He really liked me, and didn't think it was right that I was just sitting around getting pissed and didn't have any friends. We started to meet regularly, and eventually, he decided he was going to manage me. It was such a lifeline.

He introduced me to his brother, Jez Ashurst, and all these young musicians who were at least 15 years younger than me. By this time I was 39. We put a band together from Jez's old band, The Last Libertines. I began working again, just inching my nose above the parapet, playing little clubs with Jez on guitar, Dan McKinna on bass, Dave Hattee on drums, and a variety of keyboard players including Zoe Rahman, the highly-acclaimed and award-winning jazz pianist and Paul Englishby, now a feted composer and conductor.

Will turned my life around. Will loves his food and one of his best buddies was Richard Coates. Richard ran Big Night Out, a restaurant where he was the chef/owner, on Regent's Park Road, in Primrose Hill, opposite Creation Records. Everybody went there including The Gallagher brothers and all the Creation Records lot. Primal Scream's studio was across the road, so they were regular customers too. Sade ate there as well. Will and Telegram loved the place. Ironically, I was to learn that the new Virgin executives who had dropped T'Pau were also regular customers, and Richard and Will were pals with them and used to get free tickets to shows. Grrr!

Others were involved. Harry Enfield had quasi-shares in it. He used to come in with Paul Whitehouse. Harry gave Richard money to help get the place going, and Richard would repay him in food. I didn't know Richard back then, or his restaurant. I used to go to Odette's, which was another well-heeled restaurant just up the road. But once I did get to know Richard, I realised I had been walking past his door for years. The timing hadn't been right for us to meet.

Will brought Richard along to the Lord Palmerston. The Lansdowne, where Simon had worked, was right around the corner from Big Night Out. Will and Richard were keen to see what Simon Palmer was up to. He had taken quite a risk leaving the wealthy, safe and hip enclave of Primrose Hill for the outpost that was Tufnell Park. It was as if he'd gone to the Wild West Frontier.

I had a dog, a bouncy four-year-old Irish Setter called Murphy. When Will introduced me to Richard, I had Murphy with me. Richard asked: 'Is that your dog?' I said yes. Richard said he'd been feeding him chips and steak fat for weeks. Murphy would go walkabout and people would feed him titbits. Murphy had been paving the way for us to meet.

When I met Richard, for the first time since Ronnie, I felt a tingle of excitement, that frisson of first attraction. Richard had a beautiful smile and he smelled really good. I found out not only was he a brilliant chef, but he used to be a paratrooper. He was really easy to talk to and was an intoxicating blend of masculinity and sensitivity. He could cook like a dream and my God he could iron a shirt – like only a soldier can.

Richard was funny and attractive and great company, but I was still sort of seeing the drummer and Richard also had a girlfriend, who was thankfully conveniently backpacking across Australia. Richard, Will and I were in a friendship-threesome, just like I had been in with Simon and Ronnie. Three wasn't a crowd at all. We went out together a lot, got drunk, and ate too much. I had a social life again. I had some proper friends. The three of us were great mates. I hadn't laughed so much in years.

But I was still battle-weary. I didn't know what I thought about relationships anymore. Then one evening, Will came to the pub and Richard wasn't there. Will kept talking but I was distracted. I interjected: 'Where's Richard?' and Will said: 'Oh, I don't know, he's got something on. Anyway, let's talk about the band, blah, blah, blah . . .' And I pretended to listen, then I'd say: 'What has he got on?' I just couldn't focus on what Will was saying. The conversation continued, but I would just keep on bringing it back to Richard. And I suddenly realised that I missed him, and I really looked forward to seeing him. It came as an exciting and slightly troubling shock. My heart was in turmoil. I had butterflies in my stomach. I kept thinking about his girlfriend. I knew, via Will, that she was on her way back from her travels soon, I didn't really know if it was serious as Richard had never really talked about her. He knew I was seeing someone and hadn't asked me about that. Richard is very English and reserved, and that was all too personal.

I was just starting to feel alive again. Through Will I felt like I had a future. I couldn't let myself be hurt again. I couldn't get a crush on someone who had a girlfriend. And I knew he was seven years younger than me and she was 20. It was just crazy, why would he dump her for me? I was nearly 40!

The day was looming larger when Richard's girlfriend was coming back from Australia. My feelings for him were rising, coupled with a sense of panic at the possibility of not being able to see him when she got back. I sensed that Richard liked me too, but neither of us was broaching the subject for fear of the other not feeling the same. One night, the three of us went to a Thai restaurant in Crouch End. I knew if I didn't make a move soon, then it would be too late. Will was driving and offered to drop me back home. I couldn't invite Richard back as The Drummer still had a key to my house. As the meal came to a close, Will was sipping the last of his lager. The bill arrived and was duly split. I blurted out to Richard: 'I don't want to go back to my place, I want to come back to yours, how do you feel about that?' Richard simply said: 'Top!' Will burst out laughing and spat his lager over the table. Without giving away too much personal detail, we had a splendid night, interrupted only by the phone ringing at around 2am. It was his girlfriend calling from Australia. Richard did not take the call.

We quickly became inseparable. And so we began a beautiful, meaningful relationship. I knew straight away it was the real thing and that I loved him as I had loved Ronnie: truly madly, deeply.

We had a few loose ends to tie up. Richard's girlfriend came back but she'd already heard via friends that Richard had been seen around town with me. I felt bad about that because she was only young. He met her in a bar to tell her face to face. He said that the worst bit was she told him that she had really liked T'Pau!

I managed to get rid of The Drummer but he was his usual awkward self. He complained that he had always cheated on his girlfriends but had never cheated on me, and this was the thanks he got. When I asked him several times to get the rest of his stuff out of my house, he dragged his heels, so Jez and some of the band came round to give me moral support, as I finally had to say: 'It's all going on to the pavement if you don't come and take it now.' I retrieved several of my CDs from the boxes. The boys loaded him out and I slammed the door shut. Such a weight was lifted from my shoulders that I almost floated up to the ceiling. He was a conniving asshole and I was an idiot for putting up with such a bad relationship. I will never do that again.

Scarlett And Dylan

It wasn't long before Richard left his grotty flat in Willesden and moved in with me. But this time I felt no panic or regret when I saw all his boxes and cases of stuff, only excitement.

In conversation as we got to know each other, I discovered that Richard had also had a long-term relationship and had been hurt. He had had a few girlfriends. Running restaurants had meant there had been a steady flow of pretty young girls to 'interview'.

He made it clear that he didn't want to be involved in something that petered out after 18 months, and at 33 he now really wanted to have a deep relationship and have kids.

Having been positively allergic to children, astonishingly this didn't frighten me. I was not aware of the tick tock of my biological clock. Kids never ever crossed my mind. I thought they clipped your wings, messed up your career and tied you down. And I was right!

I also did not know if I could get pregnant. Despite never being able to take the pill as it made me really unwell, I had never really had a scare, and now at age 39, my ovaries could well be past their sell-by date.

Within six months I was pregnant, Richard took full credit, saying his sperm were like homing salmon.

We are not sure if Scarlett, our daughter, was conceived in sunny

Tufnell Park or beautiful Barcelona on my 40th birthday, as we were practising a lot in both places. I am pretty sure I am pregnant on the cover of Red, as my jeans felt tight and I felt queasy on the shoot and video we shot for Heart And Soul '97. I had dreadful morning sickness for five months, and no amount of eating ginger biscuits or drinking mint tea helped. I threw up morning, noon and night, only recovering when some wise soul recommended I use acupressure seasick bands on my wrists. Bingo, in one hour I was fine!

After that I absolutely loved being pregnant. I waddled about, I relaxed and let myself of the hook for a lot of things: 'Can't do that I'm pregnant,' 'I'd better eat a bit more of that I'm pregnant'.

Because of my age I was termed a 'geriatric pregnancy' – an uncharming description if ever there was one. I had to be under a consultant's care for possible pregnancy problems and chromosome anomalies, such as Down's Syndrome. Waiting for the results of all the blood tests to come back was terrifying as I was bombarded with statistics. Apparently, at 40, I ran a high chance of my baby having two heads and being green.

Ronnie reacted strangely to the news. He became very emotional when I told him I was pregnant. He was down in London with Simon and we all hooked up in Primrose Hill. Ronnie and I took a walk, and I told him my news and he got upset. He said: 'But I thought you never wanted any kids?' He'd been right. At that time in my life I didn't, and I used to be very vocal about it. I poured scorn on the whole issue in interviews. I was the new breed of woman: ambitious and tough. Women like me didn't need babies. So if Ronnie had wanted children, he must have thought he could never mention it.

Will was happy for Richard and I when we told him, but also quite annoyed as he had booked a tour to promote the album Red, that I was about to record with Jez and the band. The trouble is, there is never a right time to get pregnant, and at my age I was not in a position to hang about, so I got on with recording Red but postponed the tour. I found it really hard work recording Red. As I got bigger, I could not hold a note without almost passing out. Nor could I walk much without getting out of breath.

We thought I had developed asthma as I seemed to get breathless and tire so easily. It turned out I had anaemia. That put paid to 17 years of being a vegetarian. Richard took over, and I was made to eat medium rare steak and masses of spinach on a daily basis. Having not eaten meat for so long I did gag a bit, but I have to say, I perked up like a droopy sunflower that had just been watered. What with his 'super sperm' and getting me back on a meat diet, Richard pronounced: 'My work here is done.'

Mercifully all was alright, and although Scarlett kept us waiting for two weeks past her due date and insisted on a 24-hour labour, our beautiful little girl was born, after a lot of screaming, testicle-squeezing and swearing: 'You fucking did this to me!' by her mummy at 3.20pm on Tuesday 2nd of June 1998.

We loaded our precious cargo into the car. Richard was extremely nervous, and drove so slowly I said she would celebrate her first birthday before we got her home. Crazy as it sounds, we did not go straight home from Camden UCH but to the Lord Palmerston, and had Champagne courtesy of Simon Palmer as our daughter slept in her bassinet on a table.

When Scarlett was six months old, we went on the road. My Mum came to stay and looked after her sometimes, and other times she and Mum came on the road with me. The band were very sweet with her, and she became our mascot. I would hang her bouncer in the doorway of my dressing rooms and she would bounce around and be cuddled to bits by roadies and the band. It was all going nicely.

The gigs were small but pretty well-attended. I got a little pissed off when we played the Brannigans Sports Bars and I was billed below the chicken wings on the laminated table menus. But in the main, I was having a ball. I had lovely people in my life, a new man and a beautiful baby girl. Will managed to secure us a two-week support slot on Status Quo's European tour. That involved Mum moving into our house to look after Scarlett full-time. Scarlett was a cheerful, healthy baby with no health or feeding issues. She went easily onto formula when I stopped breast-feeding. She adored her Nan, and seemed to have no separation anxiety from me at all.

In fact, I noticed that when Mum and I were in a room with her, her eyes would follow Mum and not me. I refused to let that bother me, as it was great that Scarlett felt secure with Mum.

I thought I had everything sorted out, all my ducks lined up. I'd just pop off to Europe for a month.

I had not banked on the separation anxiety that I suffered when I was away from Scarlett, however, and I sobbed myself to sleep every night. After the first week, Richard drove across Europe to get to me with Mum and Scarlett, so I could hold my baby. I stored up her love so that I could cope with the next week away without her. Scarlett was giggly and very happy so I took solace in that. When they left, I locked myself in my dressing room and wept. I never again took such a long break from my young children. I felt physically sick if I was away from them for more than a weekend.

Ronnie and I had kept up a friendly relationship and he'd listen through things for me and give me his opinion. He'd send me good luck faxes, too, when I had gigs. On releasing Red, I didn't know what to expect. I formed my own label Gnatfish Records. The name was conceived by Will, who mockingly said I had the attention span of a gnat and the memory of a goldfish. The credible music press slagged it to the skies, to such an extent that Richard and Will told me not to read any of the reviews. I didn't. It didn't chart as we didn't get any radio play and I didn't have the money to do any promotion. There were no pluggers. So the only thing I could hope for was to sell it after the shows. And it sold really well, and all that money was mine. But it didn't get any profile, which I'd become accustomed to, and I did not like that.

Will being practical, and also having an axe to grind with the record industry, kept saying: 'But all of the money you are making is yours. You now control everything, Carol.' But all I could see was that I controlled something really small, so I was getting frustrated very quickly. And although I had had a lot of fun and thought I would be okay with it being the way it was, I wasn't. I had expectations. I couldn't help it. Creatively, it had been satisfying. I always love being in the studio, and most of the songs I was happy with: though you are never happy with an entire album, although my most recent album Pleasure And Pain is a strong contender for my favourite. Will was a manager and a trained lawyer, not an artist, and I could not get him to understand my disappointment and frustration. He also had his own agenda for wanting to exist outside of the industry, as he'd had some of his own bad experiences and was cynical.

I still felt adrift without the status of a big label and the funding and promotion they provided. I was back playing the same places I played in the early days, but just on a better fee because I'd been famous once. I tried to come to terms with it all, but found it quite hard.

It was starting to cause a problem between Will and I. Will took it very personally that I was comparing the hard work he'd done unfavourably with my achievements from the past. I was incredibly grateful for everything he'd done for me. I practically owed him my life, but I couldn't help how I felt. Things were further compounded by a week's worth of gigs in a sort of TGI joint in Madrid. It sounded so exciting to be off to Madrid, but it turned out to be a residency in a bar and chicken joint. No one really paid attention. I felt like 'the turn' and not the big star I had once been. Do I sound like a spoiled brat? I don't blame you if you think so.

The good bit was that the band were wonderful, really enthusiastic young guys who weren't out to have an argument with me every five minutes. They just wanted to play, get paid and get pissed. I liked that too, but I had experienced so much, and realised I wasn't ready to play little clubs again yet. I had not come to terms with the quality of work that was now available to me.

Will and I met for a coffee and he said: 'I don't think you want to do this anymore.' He was disappointed and upset, and commented that I was a 'glass empty sort of person' and that 'nothing would ever be enough.' We agreed to part professional company, but sadly it impacted on our friendship, as these things do. We didn't see so much of each other, which made me really sad, as it also affected his relationship with Richard. Will withdrew from our lives.

When Scarlett was three, Richard and I flew out to LA to stay with Jennie and her new partner Neal. Now free of the moody Jerry, we had great fun. I had been recording in a studio in London and got chatting

with the engineer. It turned out he was off to LA with his family at the
same time, so we exchanged numbers. He called me in LA and I arranged
for us all to get together. Jennie had suggested a day at Santa Monica Pier.
I said great, and suggested I get them to meet us there. Richard, Jennie
and Neal were all a bit unenthusiastic about it and to cut a long story
short, they were right to have reservations.

The engineer and his family were the oddest, weirdest people I'd ever
met, and I quickly regretted hooking up. We had nothing in common and
conversation was strained small talk. Their kid was bouncing off the walls
with ADHD or something. She kept eating from a bag of walnuts, saying
they were the same shape as the brain and were good for her. They clearly
didn't do much for her brain and I didn't know how to get rid of them,
and felt guilty having made the plan to meet up. I reverted to my default
setting: I just kept glugging wine and trying to chat.

Jennie suggested Richard and I take a walk along the beach and go
see The Pier, which gave us an escape route. She said she'd look after
Scarlett so that we could take some time to ourselves. Richard agreed and,
although I felt bad about leaving Jennie with The Walnuts, I agreed. So
Richard and I took a walk, and when we get beside Santa Monica Pier,
he dropped down to one knee (I thought his back had gone out), whipped
out a little box and opened it up. There was an engagement ring inside.
Richard proposed to me and was surprisingly nervous. Jennie and Neal
had been in on the plan, and they had all desperately been trying to get rid
of The Walnuts so that Richard could take me off. I felt so bad, as I nearly
ruined his masterplan. Of course I accepted. It was incredibly romantic
and emotional. We strolled back along the beach, hand in hand. Life was
beautiful. But we did have an eight-year engagement.

I was pregnant again when Scarlett was about two, but sadly I lost the
baby. It was very early on in the pregnancy. One in four pregnancies do
not make it through the first trimester. It had nothing to do with my age.

Having had a wonderful experience at UCH with Scarlett, I had a
horrible one there when I miscarried. I went along for my 12-week scan
on my own. We were old hands at it and I told Richard not to worry,
I'd go and see him later on. He was now executive chef for Belgo

Restaurants. They were at that time a very hip Belgian concept of Moules-Frites and Beer. Belgo Central was in Covent Garden, just up the road from the UCH on Gower Street. I was called in for my scan. I lay down, lifted up my top, and the doctor put the gel on my belly and started the ultrasound scan. He was initially chatty but went very quiet. Across the room a woman was sitting at a desk with a file, ready to take notes.

The doctor said: 'I am so sorry, I can see the foetus but I cannot detect a heartbeat.' I went into shock. I was speechless. I felt very pregnant, my boobs were big and I had terrible morning sickness. I felt just as I had done with Scarlett. About three weeks before, in the middle of the night, I had woken with agonising cramps that took 20 minutes to subside, but eventually they did. I had sipped some water and gone back to sleep. I didn't tell Richard. Nothing else happened, I just thought it was terrible stitch. I now realised that's when I had lost my baby.

I tried to keep calm. I was dazed by the news, and still numb, but bizarrely, I noticed that the woman taking notes across the room, on hearing what the doctor said, instantly snapped her file shut and got ready to leave the room, without looking at me to sympathise or show any consideration. She had heard it all before. I was just another statistic. I suddenly remembered that I took a fall skiing. We had already booked the trip, and then I did a pregnancy test which was positive. I did wonder if I should go, but it was really early stages, and I felt well, so we went ahead. I started to blame myself. The young male doctor took my hand, and said very firmly that under no circumstance was this my fault. I was to be taken to another room for counselling. By now the tears were coming, and I said I was worried about walking through the waiting room full of other pregnant women waiting for their scans in such a state. I asked if there was another way out. The woman with the file said: 'Just flick your fringe over your eyes.' How callous.

I was then taken to a small windowless room, and left crying on my own for an hour. I managed to get through to a colleague of Richard's, as I couldn't reach him immediately. When he got the call he raced to the hospital, but it took him 15 minutes to find me, as no-one knew where I was. The reason I still felt pregnant was because, putting it bluntly, the baby had not jettisoned so my womb and body carried on as normal. It's called a missed miscarriage. I basically had to have an abortion.

The next day we needed to regroup as a family, so we took Scarlett to St Paul's Cathedral. She was crazy about Mary Poppins and sang Feed The Birds over and over. We showed her all the pigeons like the bird lady fed on the steps of the cathedral in the film. We thought it was a nice thing to do with our sweet baby girl, for whom we were now so deeply grateful.

Scarlett promptly raced into the thronging flock and tried to kick them all.

We let the dust settle on the sadness, and even though my age was against me, we didn't try for another a baby for a while. It makes you really nervous when you have miscarried that it will happen again. The pain is unbearable. It takes a lot of courage to try again.

But about a year later, I was happily pregnant and anxious to get past my first trimester. We went privately for all the 'oh-my-God-you're-so-old' tests. Once again, we were blessed and our baby was absolutely fine. We decided to know the sex and were over the moon to be told it was boy. We had the set!

I was made aware that my placenta was low, but reassured that it would probably move out of the way as I got bigger. It didn't, and I had to be closely monitored. When I was seven months pregnant, I got up one Monday morning to get Scarlett ready for nursery. I went to the loo for my morning ablutions but my pee felt really warm. I looked down and the pan was filling up with blood. I screamed for Richard. I was in no pain. Fortunately we lived round the corner from The Whittington Hospital, in Highgate, where I was under a consultant for my pregnancy. Richard raced me up there and we ran into the maternity reception, Richard shouting: 'She's bleeding!' I was silent; my face set like stone. Inside I was panicking, thinking 'No! No! No! No! I can't lose this baby this far along.'

When my previous pregnancy terminated early it was heartbreaking, but Richard and I came to terms with it and accepted that it wasn't meant to be, and nature had taken its course. To lose a baby so far along the line, however, would have been like a death. My placenta was in the wrong place, under the baby, and it had ruptured. I was losing blood by the second. I was rushed to a ward and laid flat; mercifully the bleeding stopped, but shortly after I went into labour as all the activity in my womb told my body to start contractions. The doctors got a monitor on me and our baby boy was holding on, his heartbeat steady. I was given drugs to stop the contractions, as they did not want to bring him out so early. I was told I could not go home until the baby was born. That was devastating for Scarlett, who at only three-and-a-half was already worried about this interloper. Now, Mummy couldn't come home because of it. She became very withdrawn.

I went into labour three more times. Finally, it all settled down, but I was on strict bed rest and a date was set for my planned caesarian section as the placenta was in the way of a normal delivery.

I became quite institutionalised by being in there for so long. My days were spent lolling around having constant tests, various jabs and my blood taken. I had to have the monitor on several times a day, for an hour each time, and I listened to it with joy as the reassuring heartbeat of my son thumped its steady rhythm. I had first-class treatment from dedicated nurses and doctors.

The Whittington also served Holloway Prison, and there were several young pregnant prisoners on my ward. They had problem pregnancies too; it was the high-risk ward. They had their guards sat by their beds all day and all night, and they were loosely handcuffed at times to their beds. When they needed the loo, or to take a shower, their guards stood across the doorway so that no-one could get in or out. It felt bizarre when I was shuffling in the lunch queue, with prison guards watching us all. I began to feel I was in prison too.

After about a month, I was allowed to wheel my drip down to reception to get sweets and magazines. I once sneaked out to a nearby café with Teresa to have lunch. After almost two months, I insisted on being allowed home for a few hours with Richard, and then negotiated with my consultant for one night in my own bed. The hospital administrator was furious. She said: 'Carol, it can happen in your sleep.

You will feel no pain, and you and your baby will die in 15 minutes.' I stuck to my guns. I thought it was important for Scarlett, but I did not sleep a wink and after that night, elected to do as I was advised and always go back to the ward.

At 38 weeks, it was safe to have my boy. Dylan was delivered by C-section at 11.30am on Friday the 1st of August, 2002.

It is a strange experience, having a C- section. I was numbed but wide awake while someone cut my stomach open. Richard was going to be with me, as he had been for Scarlett's birth. I was worried about the gore, but his father had reassuringly told me that: 'He'd be OK as he'd done his butchery course at catering college.'

A green curtain was raised vertically at my chest so I could not see my stomach and the surgeon began. It felt like someone was doing the washing up violently in my stomach. Richard was squeezing my hand reassuringly but looked a bit worried. He told me, much later, that there was a bucket on the floor with a pipe in it coming from my stomach. It was filling up with blood at a terrifying rate. Dylan came out blue and silent, and our hearts almost stopped. The nurse took him and put him under a big warm light, and rubbed him hard with a towel. He drew his first breath and started crying, phew! We had not been told that this was common. A C-section baby does not go through the birth canal, which causes them to take their first breath. He was still asleep when he was born.

He started to feed immediately and I was taken to a side room. Richard's mum and dad were there pretty quickly. I was struggling to stay awake. They were across the room cooing over Dylan. I could hear them all whispering, saying: 'She's been through a lot, let her sleep.' But I was trying to talk and couldn't. I was slipping down into darkness. A nurse came by to check on me. She took my pulse and sounded the alarm. I had barely any blood pressure, and my heart was close to stopping. Rapidly they pumped me full of saline fluid to get my pulse up. Then I received four units of blood. I was as right as rain in an hour. It was strange to think how dangerous the situation was, and how quickly it was put right. But I was not out of the woods yet.

When I had been home for about two weeks the midwife came round to remove my stitches. All seemed fine, according to her. About a week later, I felt really unwell and I was running a terrible temperature, so I took a bath to freshen up. When I looked in the mirror as I dried myself, I could see that my C-section scar was breaking down. I got dressed and walked in delirium with Dylan in his buggy to The Whittington. They found my consultant and straight away she took a swab. I had MRSA in my wound. What next?! Thank the Lord that after a course of heavy-duty antibiotics, I recovered. It was a hard slog back to normality but we made it, and now we were four.

I had the great privilege a couple of years later of handing out medals to 80 blood donors on World Blood Day. Some of those men and women had donated blood 300 times. Without people like that, Dylan and I wouldn't be here.

Fucked To Death

By 2001, Richard was Executive Chef at Belgo. The restaurant group had bought The Ivy, Caprice, J.Sheekey and The Collection. They were London's high-end eateries of the day. Richard had opened a Belgo in New York, Dublin and Bristol. The company was hip, glamorous and expanding. In 1999, when Scarlett was six months old, the three of us had crammed into what was loosely called an apartment, just off Washington Square, in Manhattan, while Richard was working out there. I say loosely, as it was actually a bedroom with a tiny bathroom, and a kettle and microwave in the closet. That was the kitchen. The trip coincided with the horrific New York blizzards. Manhattan is boiling in the summer and biblically cold in the winter. Richard was working round the clock, and I literally could not go outside in those minus temperatures with my baby,

so I watched a lot of TV on my own and ate a lot of Chinese take-out.
Mum came out for a week when the weather picked up, and finally we got
to enjoy the Big Apple. We had a local bar in The Village. I made a few
calls about my album Red, jogged a few memories, and managed to get
VH1 to come and film me at the glamorous opening of Belgo. They sent a
film crew to follow me around for the day, just like Kim Kardashian, and
interviewed me about the album. I asked if they could let me know the
transmission date and they duly did. I was slotted into a series called 'One
Hit Wonders: Where are they now?' Bugger.

Whenever they opened a new restaurant there was a big press
launch and party. At the opening of Belgo Sud, in Ladbroke Grove, I got
talking to theatrical agent Paul Telford. We chatted about acting and the
possibility of me looking at other things. I signed up to his agency and
was quickly auditioned for various things.

I played a distraught mother whose child had impaled himself on a
pencil in BBC One's Doctors. Then I was a singer with a man's voice –
they dubbed a bloke over my voice – in Star, a kids' drama with Nicolas
Hoult. I played an American corporate bitch in Running Time, the first
ever interactive movie, where the public decided the script outcome. It
was BAFTA-nominated. I auditioned for several West End productions
such as Chicago, Blood Brothers, Taboo, Jesus Christ Superstar and We
Will Rock You. I always got a second or even a third callback, but never
got the part. Just like the old days, I was never quite right. 'We've gone in
another direction' is the stock answer from the casting directors. Which
way, I can go that way too?

I read unsuccessfully for Stephen Frears. That was utterly terrifying
as I could tell straight away he was deeply unimpressed. When I arrived at
his house he was on the T'Pau website looking at my posing, beautifully-
lit, pop star promo shots. He then looked at me and remarked ungallantly:
'Is that really you?' I must have looked a bit shit that day.

I was excited to learn from my agent that I had secured a small part in
a film called Nine Dead Gay Guys – a dark, comedy, gay, murder mystery
starring Michael Praed and Stephen Berkoff, and Marillion frontman,
Fish. I was to play Berkoff's wife. It was just a little cameo role, one

scene. I met with the director but did not need to audition. I arrived at the flat being used as the set. The crew were all young kids around 20 and were so excited I was on the shoot; many of them had brought their old T'Pau albums to be signed. I was sitting down and signing albums, and having pictures taken with the crew. I was the Queen for a day again!

Stephen walked in, saw the fuss being made of me and said sharply: 'Oh fine don't get up!' Quickly, the crew dispersed and I stood and walked forward to shake hands. He was clearly annoyed that someone else was the centre of attention. He did not shake my hand or acknowledge me, and flounced off into wardrobe. The crew and I looked at each other and winced.

There was a production manager called Peter on set, whose job it was to smoothe Stephen's feathers and placate him. Stephen had to wear a waistcoat in our scene with no shirt underneath, and he was very concerned that his physique looked okay. Ever the team player, I joined with Peter to reassure Stephen that he looked great. We fussed around him with the wardrobe girls, telling him the colour made his eyes pop and all that. He began to defrost with me, but I had to absolutely play the admiring ingénue. My costume consisted of a very skimpy nightie! It turned out that our scene involved Stephen shagging me to death, and we did a really convincing job and broke the headboard on the bed. My character did not have a name but as Stephen reached his screen climax, he called me Edith. I was looking so hot in that nightie; and a hottie would not have been called bloody Edith! He gave me an unsexy name on purpose.

My main concern at the time was that I had hideous bunions: don't worry, I've had the op since. Obviously Nine Dead Gay Guys was going to be a massive hit. I would be launched into a huge Hollywood career – and everyone would see my feet. Getting rigorously rogered to death and trying to hide your bunions is not an easy task I can tell you.

The film was an utter turkey and was unilaterally slagged off. Nobody got to see my feet.

Several years later I met Stephen at 'An Audience With Neil Diamond.' He remembered me well and was genuinely charming company. We joked how proud my Mum must have been that I was shagged to death by such a great actor. I saw no trace of the diva I had worked with that day, and can only assume that when he's acting he gets very intense, or was grumpy that he'd committed to what he could already sense was a very, very bad film.

Finally I got a lucky break and successfully auditioned for a play called Mum's The Word. It was a comedy about being a mum and all the trials and tribulation that involves. We had to be mums to attend the audition and I read and got the part. It was an ensemble cast, meaning equal billing, starring Jennie Eclair, Patsy Palmer, Cathy Tyson, the Canadian writer of the play and actress Barbara Pollard, yours truly and Shakespearian lovie Imogen Stubbs, who was at that time married to Trevor Nunn, the legendary theatre, TV and film director. I could not get over my being cast with such heavyweight actors such as Cathy and Imogen, and hugely popular stars like Patsy and Jennie.

By the time of our first read through, about three months before we opened at The Albery, on St Martin's Lane, I knew all my lines. I learned that it's called 'being off the book'. I had to learn a whole lot of new jargon for the acting world. Drying has nothing to do with bath time but means forgetting your lines; corpsing is not a love of necrophilia but means laughing; and The Dickies was not at all what I thought. 'He can still do The Dickies darling'.

My bubble was soon burst, sadly. Firstly, at the press launch and photocall, Imogen was very off hand with me. She was kneeling on the floor reading something. I saw her look up at me, but she quickly looked back down. I had met everyone else previously but Imogen had been away, and we had not yet met. I sensed an immediate friction coming entirely from her. It was distressing, in truth, because I'd been beyond excited to meet her. I had a bad feeling. You know when someone has taken an instant dislike to you; you don't know why, but you know there's nothing you can do about it.

Imogen had dyed her waist-length blonde hair red. The director said: 'Oh … Imogen I hired you as a blonde.' Patsy Palmer and I were natural redheads, and had both coincidentally cut our famous long red locks short.

Imogen didn't look at him and just muttered: 'I fancied a change.' It was bizarre.

As our work progressed, we rehearsed near Shoreditch in 'a space'. As I said, I was word perfect as I was terrified. I had driven Richard mad, making him go over and over my lines with me. I have always had a bit of a rubbish memory, so I was very worried, plus Dylan was only six-months-old. I was sleep-deprived and paranoid about forgetting lines. I was having anxiety dreams where I was naked on the stage and couldn't remember my lines. I couldn't get off the stage, and everyone was laughing and pointing. I thought I'd be welcomed for being 'off the book'. But I learned that I was perceived as a goodie two shoes and a bit smug for knowing all my lines too far in advance. Everyone else was still on the book. I looked like the teacher's pet.

When we broke for coffee, I was walking back from the kitchen and Imogen was walking towards me. She said: 'Well done Carol, you know all your lines and I must admit I thought you were going to be crap.' That's a quote. I have never forgotten it. I felt blindsided by her. I replied: 'And what would bring you to that conclusion?' She said harshly 'speak as I find' and flounced off. I was shaking inside. I realised this was going to be a horrible experience if she was going to try and undermine me at every turn.

I told my agent, who was sadly not surprised. I came to learn that everyone else was theatrically trained, even comedienne, Jennie Eclair had been to drama school in Manchester. She was in the club. I was perceived as an impudent interloper: 'So you think you can come from your little rock band and share a stage with trained actors! I went to RADA you know!'

All of the cast were nice to me and I liked them, particularly Jennie, who is hysterical. But I saw quickly that they had to pick a side. Imogen clearly didn't like me, and she and husband Trevor Nunn were very influential. A couple of the cast kept so close to her that they almost wore her as a hat, if you get my drift. I could do no good, she also complained I posed too much in the posters. And she was probably right about that, as I had been pouting and posing in my posters for years. It was a hard habit to break! Pop stars pose!

Dyeing her long hair red was bizarre as it was my trademark, and she knew it. She had never been red before or since, to my knowledge. For my part, I was devastated to be so dismissed by someone I had admired and was hoping to learn from as a fledgling actor, that I would go home and cry. The resident director observed it all and saw me withdraw into myself. She said: 'Don't you dare let anyone beat you down.' But it was hard, I was in a new medium, and I was really nervous every night. One night I did dry and it is just awful, you want to die! I wasn't on home turf, and it was made clear to me that I didn't rule the roost. I felt very isolated.

The opening press night was star-studded. I invited all my pals, including my friend Kim Wilde. Kate Moss was apparently in my dressing room looking to say 'hi', but I had taken Kim to the bloody toilet and missed meeting her. It was so exciting, the audience roared with laughter and I thought this acting malarkey was easy: 'We're a hit!'

One of the cast said to me: 'You know you've got to do it all again tomorrow, don't you?'

We then went straight into the run of eight shows a week, with a lot of very empty matinees. I hated doing two performances and I hate doing two music sets. I give my all in a performance and then what? Again? It's like coming – I'm done, I'm spent, I need a pizza now and a nap.

At a drinks party in the theatre one night, China In Your Hand came on the playlist. Patsy Palmer started singing loudly and told me how great my song was. Imogen said disingenuously and very theatrically: 'Oh is this yoooooo? I didn't realise this was yooooo!' Yeah right.

On the way home, Richard was pissing himself laughing. We both knew she knew my song. It was then that I finally found her funny. She was jealous, it was that simple. After that I relaxed and ignored her. The other girls in the cast started going out to tea with her every afternoon. I didn't feel welcome and decided to keep my distance. Richard's office was right around the corner in The Ivy, so I would meet him there after matinee. Patsy sometimes would organise a dance lesson for us all at Pineapple with Louis Walsh. Patsy also turned 30 that year, and threw a big swanky party, which was very top drawer with lots of famous faces and paparazzi. We took rooms with her at The St Martin's Lane Hotel. Patsy liked a very good time, as did Richard and I. We all misbehaved quite a bit. I learned a few years later that she was fighting a lot of demons back then. Patsy always seemed to get 'gifted' by designers. We all had to do interviews to promote the play. Patsy mentioned she loved Agent Provocateur Lingerie in a fashion piece, and a box arrived for her at the stage door. It cost a bloody fortune. I did a more mumsy health piece in a mag and mentioned my anaemia. That week I got a huge box of iron supplements sent to me. I just was not savvy enough in interviews. I never talked about the right things. By the way, if anyone from Prada is reading this . . .

During that time Imogen's then-husband, Trevor Nunn, got knighted. I joked to Imogen that we'd have to call her Lady Nunn. She replied: 'Too right.' I think she meant it.

Keeping myself to myself, and not rising to the bait or showing when I was hurt seemed to do the trick, but I did feel lonely. About a month in, Imogen started to walk towards me in the green room and she never came over to me. I braced myself. What the fuck did she want?

She said: 'Trevor was in the house last night – he thought you were rather good.' WOW! Sir Trevor thought I was rather good, fab news, I could see myself starring in all his musicals. That didn't happen alas. I was also annoyingly relieved that Imogen was being nice to me, like when the school bully throws you a crumb of affection or just doesn't hit you. It was such a relief!

Shortly after, she invited me into the Tea Party Gang. So things improved and we were reasonably amicable colleagues. The play got panned and we only ran for four months. The theatre critic Nicolas De Jong thought it part of the dumbing down of theatre, and queried what a great actress like Imogen was doing in such a lightweight piece. I had reasonable reviews as a newcomer.

About a year later, I was at ITV on The Southbank, in reception waiting to take a meeting, when off in the distance I saw Imogen. I pretended not to see her and look preoccupied with very important stuff. The cry came loudly across the room: 'Carol! Carol Decker! Is that yooooo?' She stalked over and plonked herself down on the sofa. She was also at ITV for a meeting and had a streaming cold. I gave her a throat sweet. Imogen mused: 'Such a shame about Mum's The Word. We did have such fun didn't we.'

As well as doing a bit of acting in 2001, I got a phone call from promoter Tony Denton, asking me if I would appear on an '80s tour with Paul Young, Heaven 17, Kim Wilde, Go West and a few others, including Curiosity Killed The Cat from back in my Chris Cooke days. We would be playing the arenas around the UK. Yippee. I would be on the stage at Wembley again.

I had to sing four or five songs. I got paid a decent amount of money, and my husband and my daughter were waiting in the wings. I loved it. They were big crowds and I was back on a big stage where I felt I belonged. I really didn't mind that I wasn't headlining. I didn't want the pressure. We were all the big hitters of our day, so we all got a really good reception. I was going down a storm and I felt I was in good company.

That was the start of the '80s renaissance. After a decade in the cold in the '90s, when none of us could get arrested, it felt great to be warmly received again. We shared a house band made up of first-rate musicians. They worked hard to get all our authentic '80s keyboard sounds and effects. With two keyboard players in the set-up, many of the parts that Michael had overdubbed on the records could now be played live. We didn't have to choose between them and compromise. After the Wembley show, my mother said she had never heard the songs sound so good. It was closer to the record.

Those shows were also very compatible with my new family life. I could take Scarlett with me. I was on stage for about 25 minutes then I was propping up the bar with Richard, by 8.30pm, watching the show. The Here And Now tours continued for a further five or six years. We started to travel abroad with the shows too. I have always likened these sorties to an '80s pop star school trip. It was so amusing to see people stare at us, open-mouthed, as a gaggle of their childhood favourites stalked through the airport terminal.

I'd often buddy up with Kim Wilde. Although we had worked

together a little down the years, we became good pals doing the Here And Now shows. We have a lot in common. Our kids are a similar age. We had so many shared experiences in the business and stories to tell each other. We both had Scouse mothers, too. Mine was a Littlewoods songster and Kim's mum Joyce, was a Vernon's Girl.

Kim also lived not too far from my Auntie Marie, in Hertfordshire. When my Mum had a mild stroke in 2001, my aunt looked after her as both my brother and I had small children, and couldn't cope with Mum at that time. Marie ran a private care home so was all set up to care for the infirm. I would give Kim a buzz if I was visiting Mum and swing by on the way back. I would take Scarlett to my Auntie Marie's in Stevenage and we'd spend the day, but it was always upsetting to see Mum not quite herself.

Her stroke had more of an impact on her personality. She could be quite grumpy and would often get hold of the wrong end of the stick. She also became very critical and argumentative. She recovered from the milder physical symptoms pretty quickly. But it was exhausting pretending to be cheerful when you're worried, and frankly, Mum's behaviour was challenging. Sadly things got worse as she got older. So it was lovely to decompress at Kim's place with a glass and a gab. She was a good listener. Well she had to be as I talk a lot.

Kim always takes the piss out of my hypochondria. If we talk on the phone, she says: 'Okay you've got five minutes on your ailments.' She's thrown some bloody amazing parties too. One New Year we were staying at Kim's, she was throwing a big New Year's bash and lots of her music pals were coming. Kim lives in Hertfordshire. For those not driving, Welwyn was suggested as a good place to get the train to, followed by a cab to Kim's.

Shortly after we'd all sung Auld Lang Syne at midnight, the phone rang and it was Steve Strange. He'd got the train from his home in Wales to Welling, near Dartford. We were all in bits. Undaunted, Steve got several more trains back to Welwyn and then a cab to Kim's and arrived at about 3am. We were all starting to fade by then. He'd been travelling all day and had spent a fortune. He then said casually: 'I don't know why

I did that as I used to live near Welwyn.'

About six years ago several of us, including Go West, Martin Fry of ABC and Steve went on a trip out to Lille to perform on a big Belgian pop show. We all met at the Eurostar terminal at St Pancras at about 8am. Most of us lived in or around London, but Steve was living back in Wales in Bridgend, which was three-and-a-half hours away. He'd had to get up at the crack of dawn to get there for the 8am train. The tour manager asked for all our passports, Steve did not have his. He said when he got in his cab he'd asked his driver, who was foreign, if you needed a passport to go to Europe now that we were in the EU. The driver said he didn't think so. That was good enough for Steve, and he didn't bring it, not even as a precaution. He had to drive all the way back to Bridgend, get his passport, and drive back to St Pancras and get a later train. That was 10 hours in a cab, then the train, then another cab to the studio. I was exhausted on his behalf. Of course, it was entirely the bloody cab driver's fault, giving him misinformation.

Growing up in the sticks I never knew Steve in his heyday at The Blitz Club but I knew his importance in the New Romantic Movement. He was part of that cultural shift with his band Visage and other über fashionable bands like Spandau, Culture Club, Adam And The Ants et al. We went through a brief time of being on the same bill or TV show, and he was a real sweetheart but so scatty, it was painful at times. Once we had to share a cab to a TV show or some such. When he got in, he sounded like he'd just had some teeth out and it looked like his mouth was frozen with dental block. He was also dribbling a bit out of one side. He mumbled an apology in his lovely soft Welsh accent: 'Thorry Cawol, I can't weally thpeak, I've jutht had my lipz done.' His lips looked like two pink pillows. I was crying with laughter. I have such happy memories of the few years I knew him.

Richard and I had both been living in London for a long time and had loved every minute of it, but something had changed now we had two kids. Everything started to feel a bit of a hassle: the crowded Tubes and busy streets that had for so long excited me, now seemed to be on top of me. Richard was also tiring of corporate restaurant life. Belgo had been floated on the stock market, and was no longer the avant garde independent place to work that it had once been. Now there were shareholders to please, and Richard was spending most of his time cutting costs and staff to maximise profits. That was not making him happy: he may be in business but he remains a creative person.

Belgo had been an exciting place to work. It was the brainchild of Denis Blais, an eccentric French Canadian entrepreneur, art collector and artist manager. Ron Arad, the award-winning industrial architect had designed the first two restaurants. Belgo had been a cool and unique experience for customers and staff alike. As executive chef, Richard's job covered everything from hiring staff, designing new dishes and maintaining the authenticity of the concept to moving it forward within those ideals. He also had to literally go pick up the mussels sometimes. On a few occasions, I accompanied him to Heathrow to pick up mussels flown in from around the world. If Red Tide bacteria hit the sea from a usual supplier in, say, Wales or Ireland, then panicky phone calls were made to get them from Canada or Holland, or Norway or vice versa. In the crazy world of fresh seafood, it could all change overnight, and with Belgo shifting 15 tons of mussel and two tons of lobster a week, those problems had to be solved quickly.

It was a challenging but rewarding job because pride was the motivating force, rather than just making money. But Denis had sold up to a massively successful, but more straightforward profit-driven businessman, and things were not the same. Richard was getting disillusioned at work so decided, with another colleague, to leave and have his own place again. He found The Cherry Tree, a charming, 600-year-old pub in Stoke Row, four miles outside Henley-on-Thames. It needed a lot of renovation. There were also stables to convert into letting rooms. It didn't take long before Richard had The Cherry Tree in the Michelin guide for his food, and had AA rosettes for the accommodation as well. Word spread and amongst his regular customers were film director Paul Greengrass, Phillip Schofield, actor John Hannah and Formula 1 supremo Ross Braun, who brought in Michael Schumacher. Richard commuted for two exhausting years.

In 2005 Richard and I decided to take the plunge and move to Henley. Scarlett was now seven and Dylan coming up to three. I found it a hard decision to make. I had grown up in small rural towns and couldn't wait to get the hell out of them and see the bright lights. We moved house on September 9th, 2005, on the day before my 48th birthday. Richard had to go straight to work. After he left I sat on a packing crate and cried. The move had been fraught with tension; our buyer in London was an asshole who tried to knock 5k off the agreed price in the last 24hours and threatened to pull out of the sale. He was an arrogant city trader who thought he was being clever, but he had no idea how stubborn Richard and I can be. We held our nerve and told him to fuck off. We counter threatened not to move out the next morning. The removals company was booked, all of our belongings were in boxes, and we were spending the last night on mattresses on the floor. Scarlett also had now left her junior school in Highgate, and I was told she could not simply rejoin her class but would have to go on the waiting list to get back in. It was nightmare. In the end it all went grudgingly through but it took its toll on us.

The next morning our solicitor called and told me all the funds had gone into my account. It was no longer my home. The arrogant trader was waiting impatiently at the bottom of the steps with his snotty French wife. We shut the door and handed him the key. But I felt rushed out, and left without saying a proper goodbye to my house. Richard had lived there with me for the last seven years, but I was leaving my home of 20 years and I'd lived several lives there. I had shared the house with Ronnie, hoping for an exciting new life together in the big city. I had shared it with several itinerant friends when Ronnie left. I had shared it with the awful drummer when it felt like a prison and finally, and so very happily, I shared it with Richard and my children, when the house came alive again. I had been incredibly happy there, then incredibly sad and then incredibly happy again. For over a year I dreamed, frequently, that I was walking through it.

Simon Palmer left The Lord Palmerston shortly after – I fear he stopped turning a profit after I left.

It was an exciting and nerve-racking time. The house was a bit of a project but we loved doing it up, picking the colours, shopping for bathrooms and new furniture. I immersed myself in design magazines and TV shows like Grand Designs. Sarah Beeny became my heroine. I had to get the kids into nursery and school. I knew nobody, but a lot of them knew me. I was overly-smiley in the playground, hoping not to intimidate the other mums or appear standoffish or entitled in any way. There was a lot of whispering until they got used to me. Nobody noticed or cared in London, plus I had lived in my 'manor' for 20 years, so I was just a neighbour.

To cut a long story short, we have, at the time of writing this book, been here for 10 years and only now do I feeling like I fit in here – and that's been down to me. Although I wanted to make the move, I joke that I left my nail marks in the M40 the day we moved. I was really scared about the change and I did find the adjustment hard. I loved the anonymity of London. In a small town, everybody knows your business. There is, of course, a self-appointed hierarchy and Old Guard in a place like Henley-On-Thames, which I loathe as I hate snobbery. Although I have absolutely enjoyed the perks of being a little bit famous, I am not an elitist. There are also of course lovely, normal people in Henley, but it's taken me years to work out how to live here.

In 2006, after 10 months of living in Henley, we decided to get married. I made myself somewhat unpopular with my mother's family as we invited only 80 friends and immediate family. My mother being one of seven, and from a Catholic background, meant that I do have a shed-load of aunts, uncles and cousins that I have not seen in years. I am a really practical person; I didn't mean to offend or hurt my relatives but we have nothing to do with each other's lives and I wanted to spend the day with the people I feel most close to. A couple of my aunties gave Mum a really hard time on the phone, as they felt very slighted.

We were also arranging the wedding ourselves. We had discussed getting married many times but always talked ourselves out of it. We'd seen other friends get married and the arrangements seemed so stressful: Who should come, who should sit where, who gets on with whom and so on. And the expense always seemed shocking.

We are not religious, nor do we care for social mores, so we did not feel in any way that our relationship was not a true one. I hate fuss and would have run away with the kids and had a beach wedding, but Richard felt that would have been a hollow victory. I had a gig coming up abroad and we discussed Richard catching up with me with the kids and making it a bit of a holiday. We discovered that we had misinformation about the rights of a father over his children if he is not married. Richard could not take them out of the country without a lot of paper work being signed by me. Our love for each other and our children was a given. So for the most prosaic and unromantic of reasons, we decided to wed.

We got married in the local register office, which had a pretty room. Richard's restaurateur life meant he was able to source all the food, getting a great deal on fabulous food like lobster and organic steak, instead of the awful unimaginative wedding food that most caterers provide. Our close friend Andres Blais provided a cocktail bar and mixologist as his gift. A mum at the kids' junior school was taking a floristry course, so she did our flowers at a knockdown price so she could have us on her CV. My Mum paid her bill as her gift to us. We hired our staff and a former chef from The Cherry Tree as waiters and grill jockey.

We had our reception in the garden and prayed for it to stop raining, as we had bought three large gazebos but had no hard flooring. The rain was torrential here in June 2006, I will never forget it. The day before our wedding we were looking at a sodden garden. We did not have a plan B, where would everyone sit? Lorraine Milligan, my friend and make-up artist whose late grandparents had owned our house for over 40 years, said to me that June 27th (our wedding date), was also the wedding date of her grandparents. She'd said it was always red hot and they always had a massive garden party. So by that logic, it would be okay: Brian and Joy would make it so. The odd thing was that out of the four dates the register office had offered us, we completely unknowingly had picked June 27th, Brian and Joy's wedding date. You can call it a coincidence, but I prefer to think Brian and Joy influenced us.

During the first year of living here, the living room door would open on its own regularly at night. It is on a magnetic catch and it would just unclick and open wide. I would say: 'Hi Brian.' Richard says it was just a draught, but it stopped happening after the first year. I think they approved of us in the house and finally left.

On the night of June 26th it was still pouring down. It was a washout. We had to be up at 6am on June 27th, the day of our wedding, to get things ready. When we did, there was a clear blue sky with not a cloud insight.

We were getting married at 11am. At 9am, I started to get ready with the help of my friends, Jackie and Jennie. I surprised everybody by wearing an ivory wedding dress and not a leather jacket and Levis. Jackie's partner David Hartfield, our friend and the organiser of the Rewind Festival, drove us down and back in his old Rolls Royce with Champagne supplied! My brother gave me away. Richard had compiled a playlist that included Billy Idol's White Wedding as I walked into the room. There was no dirge-like Wedding March here.

As well as our families, we couldn't have wished for a better turnout of old friends. Simon and Ronnie came from Monmouth with their ladies. Jez and the band were there. Richard's mates from Coulsdon in Surrey came mob-handed. Richard's mum was so relieved we were finally married; she'd tried to be modern about it bless her.

Tim Burgess, T'Pau's original drummer came over from Canada. Jennie, Neal and their son Max flew in from LA. It was a snapshot of our lives.

To have our children present was a joy. Scarlett and Dylan handed us our rings. It was so moving that they were part of the wedding, it made it about the four of us, and I highly recommend it that way round. Dylan was only three-and-a-half and announced he needed a poo very loudly in the middle of the ceremony. Jackie had to race him out and they both missed the 'I do's.'

Our dear friends Marcus, the set designer on Hot Fuzz, Shaun Of The Dead and many more great movies, and his wife Natalie, who are always late, arrived at the register office as we were all leaving.

Back at the house we had a high-end but very informal BBQ of lobster and steak, with fabulous sides and salads all prepared by Richard that morning before he jumped into his suit and married me! Champagne, seriously strong cocktails, beer and wine flowed and everyone ended up in the pool in various stages of undress. Dylan had innocently disrobed to swim and did another poo, this time in the pool. Everyone around him screamed and shot out of the water vertically. It eventually got so hot that three of our guests got sunstroke.

There was of course, as in all good weddings, lots of laugher, two women had a big argument, the tactful ejection of a very drunk person into a cab, some tears and some vomiting. In the morning we discovered we had a broken sofa!

The bride and groom fell straight to sleep that night.

Take That, Barlow

By now my work consisted largely of '80s tours and concerts. I spent four years doing endless '80s shows and only a handful of gigs with my own band. Given the arrival of Scarlett and Dylan, it made for a much easier way of working. To go on tour with my own band, I have to put in a lot of shows to make it financially worthwhile; something that business experts call economies of scale. But when the kids were young, I did not want to be out on the road all the time. The Here And Now tours and big outdoor events, such as Rewind Festival and latterly the Let's Rock shows, worked wonderfully for me. Most of the artists use the house band, as opposed to their own band, to cut down on dead stage time with changeovers. Those house bands frequently feature top players, so the quality is exceptional. I also enjoy the luxury of having two keyboard players and a sax, which I can't afford in my own set up. And the social side has been great, too. I have become pretty good pals with quite a few of my peers.

Over the last 15 years, I have toured with and appeared alongside Paul Young, ABC, Nick Heyward, Kim Wilde, Belinda Carlisle, Heaven 17, Toyah, Go West, Human League, OMD, Hazel O'Connor, China Crisis, Cutting Crew (again, all those years since our hits' days), Gloria Gaynor, Billy Ocean, Hall and Oates, Starship, Peter Hook, Eddie Reader, Boy George, Tony Hadley, the lovely Jason Donovan and Bananarama. The list goes on and on. There is the odd diva still clinging on to their ego, and thinking they are above the rest of us – yeah you, Hall and Oates with your 'closed stage' – but in the main, the atmosphere backstage at those events is very pleasant and convivial, with lots of showbiz hugs, catching up and a nice drink later.

I relaxed into those shows and started to go where the work took me. There was no longer any point in harping back to the past. I did some amazing things with Ronnie and T'Pau, but those days were over, and I enjoyed moving on. I also got a TV agent and started to enjoy appearing on the odd game show. I used to love pub quizzes and games like Trivial Pursuit, so my general knowledge was sort-of okay. I usually found my way to the right answer more by process of elimination rather than by real knowledge; but as long as the answer is right, that's just fine. After all, I passed my 11-Plus. My tried and trusted method of: 'I-know-it's-not-that-so-it-has-to-be-one-of-those-two-and-that-one-doesn't-feel-quite-right-so-I'll-go-for-that,' has stood me in good stead. It got me into grammar school.

The scariest show I appeared on was The Weakest Link with Anne Robinson. Back in 2002, the show was at its height. I was about five months pregnant with Dylan when I was asked to appear. Anne was at her scariest, and she would appear in a shaft of light as though she had been beamed down from The Starship Enterprise. She would be ruthlessly sarcastic and condescending to the contestants. I was really quite nervous when I arrived at the studio, as my surging pregnancy hormones meant I couldn't think straight anyway. I was afraid I would have one of those days where I couldn't remember my own name and look idiotic on national TV. Anne did not meet us before the show but kept up her aloof, scary-vampire-in-a-leather-coat persona. She appeared, suddenly as the cameras rolled, like Nosferatu, and sort of called us all 'has-beens'. Then she demanded that we all justify our existence and our place on her show. I was terrified of her, and Dylan started kicking me really hard whenever the loud 'DAH DAH DAH DAH 'music played. I didn't do too badly on my answers. All I ever hope for is not to be first out, and I survived into the final rounds; I was hanging on in there right up to the penultimate game. But I can't claim to have been the most strategic player. On The Weakest Link we had to accumulate money for our chosen charity and say: 'bank' when we'd got enough. I really didn't understand when I was supposed to shout out 'bank' and due to my poor grasp of numbers I developed 'bank' Tourette's and just shouted it randomly. Suzi Quatro and Lesley Garrett voted me out because of that, and I had to do the walk of shame across the floor. Cows!

The Weakest Link wasn't the only show to welcome me aboard. I also featured on Celebrity Pointless, appearing on it twice, and winning with Paul Young. On that show you have to give a brief biography of yourself, on camera, to the hosts Alexander Armstrong and Richard Osman and the audience. Unfortunately, Dave Hill from Slade and Sheila Ferguson from The Three Degrees did not understand the concept of 'brief', and thought it meant explaining their lives in real time. We were standing at our podiums on set, my back was killing me, and I could see the other contestants' eyes glazing over and starting to sway from side-to-side slightly as they prattled on. I think Dave had got as far as 1982 and Richard Osman had to stop him.

The TV work kept on coming and I did a couple of music-related shows. In 2005, I appeared/competed on Hit Me Baby One More Time. The premise was that a selection of artists had to sing their biggest hit and a contemporary cover of the day. Contestants included Nick Heyward, Belinda Carlisle, Mica Paris and Shakin' Stevens. We competed each week, and the public voted who to keep in. I got through to the final singing China and Jamelia's recent hit Superstar. As part of the show, ITV recorded interviews with everyone's families who had to big-up their singing loved one and say why we should win. It was a popular prime time show, and I got into a position where I was a pretty strong favourite to win. As the show reached its climax, all of the artists huddled around the backstage TV monitor watching our families praise our efforts. I had not seen the VT that Richard, my husband, had filmed and as I tuned in for the first time, I stood next to my rival, Shakin' Stevens. As my turn to go back on stage approached, they ran Richard's interview where he not only told the world how fabulous I was and why I should totally win, but also went on to expand on how shit he thought Shaky was. I wanted the floor to open up and swallow me: I was standing right next to the guy. Shaky looked at the floor and walked away. When Richard came backstage he was beetroot red and mortified. As a former punk and massive Stiff Little Fingers and Stranglers fan, Richard was never going to be Shaky fan but he didn't realise they would keep that comment in. Shaky went on to win. At the finale, he had to walk through us all as we queued in the corridor and applauded him like a football player going on to the pitch. He and his wife looked directly at Richard and me, and smirked the winner's smirk. It was our turn to look at the floor.

I had a spot of fun on Celebrity Mastermind when my specialist subject was Tina Turner. I got a call from the producer because they had a drop-out and needed me in at 24-hours' notice. I had been quite the Tina fan in my youth, so I dusted off an old unofficial autobiography that was on our book shelves, and revised all day. I turned into a proper old skool swat, if only I'd put that much effort into my A Levels. Once again, I did okay and didn't disgrace myself, but I didn't quite win either. I gave the rugby player Austin Healey a huge leg-up by stupidly stage-whispering the answers to a few of his questions into Nick Hancock's ear when I was off stage. When Austin came out of the chair, he thanked me as he said he'd gone blank but he'd overheard me. Nick Hancock, by the way, was a seriously clever egg-head and lovely bloke to boot.

The point of doing those shows was to keep my face around and, to be honest, they are mostly great fun too. The most exhausting show I did was Just The Two Of Us. It was a short-lived series lasting only two seasons, and was a sort-of Strictly Come Singing. A professional singer had to teach a non-singing celebrity to sing, and then compete against the others. I was allocated the then-little-known, Gregg Wallace, now of MasterChef fame. We had to be introduced on camera as a surprise to each other. I struggled to hide the fact that I had no idea who he was, and I looked into his eyes and instantly got bad vibes. Our auras clashed in an instant.

I realised that I knew Gregg from his Radio 4 programme, Veg Talk. Being a foodie's wife, I'd listened to it while I was on the road and to be fair to Gregg, he's a man who genuinely does know his onions. But I was hoping for better. Beverley Knight got Brendan Cole. And I was hoping to be a bit of a power couple with someone like that. At the very least, I'd hoped to have a top laugh. At the time of the show, Gregg was slowly breaking into TV, and he was so nervous that he tended to constantly overplay his hand. He's got a market background so he acted constantly like a barrow boy. His constant diatribe made him sound like he was still selling veg at Smithfield Market: we just couldn't shut him up. He was showing off constantly, telling crap, unfunny jokes and generally wearing us all down. The crew and I used to brace ourselves for his arrival. But that attempt at being the 'cheeky chappy' was a front, in my opinion. I tried to get on with Gregg and persuade myself that he was just being Gregg-arious and ebullient. But in truth, I found him a bit belligerent.

Gregg also couldn't carry a tune in a bucket. He had no sense of melody, and he couldn't remember whatever I taught him. We rehearsed at my house in my music room. They furnished us with a pianist and a musical director to assist, but Gregg could not recall a note within five minutes of singing it. Singing is not something I have to remember, I just do it naturally. So I found Gregg's lack of ability very alien. I guess he might have said the same of me, had the tables been turned: I can't cook, it's something I have no instinct for. Although Gregg's lack of ability was hugely challenging, I did not hold it against him, but his attitude drove me nuts. Eventually I asked him to stop mucking about, to stop holding court and start to concentrate. He didn't like it and got way too close to me, an inch from my nose, right 'up in my grill'. We exchanged words and Gregg proceeded to say that he had not asked me to change who I was, so why should I ask him? I replied: 'I have changed who I am, Gregg. I'm not a natural teacher or a patient person and I am struggling with you, but I'm doing my very best to hide all that and get on with my job.' He backed down and we worked together under sufferance.

I was sure he was simply trying to deflect from the fact that he was embarrassed and out of his depth. After a week, I never wanted to see him again for the rest of my life, much less have to work with him.

Needless to say, we went out in the first round Singing Blame It On The Boogie, A Jackson Five smash, in front of Tito Jackson, who was on the judging panel. Tito was polite but not impressed.

Another one of the judges was Stewart Copeland, the taciturn drummer with The Police. Although I had not met him in the past, I knew all about Stewart. His brother Miles had managed me, and his other brother, Ian, was my agent. I had friends who'd worked for The Police too, and the fights between him and Sting were legendary. I'd heard all the stories. He was always portrayed as argumentative and difficult, but astonishingly talented. Despite what I'd heard, I loved his band and was very keen to meet him. I knew his family, I had all The Police albums and I had toured Canada supporting their guitarist Andy Summers. I figured we'd have so much to talk about, even though I was shocked to see him on our show. After all, Stewart was hardly Mr Saturday Night. He certainly didn't need the money or that type of profile.

Stewart annihilated Gregg to the extent that even I felt sorry for him. When Gregg went out on stage he instantly started to sweat profusely under the lights, and his suit was soaked in seconds. Needless to say, his vocals were ear-wateringly bad. But to give him his due, he gave it his best shot. We had to do a 'Sing Off' with the other lowest scorers and we were voted out by the public. Stewart was so mean that I flipped him the bird on camera.

I was asked to stay on the show, not to compete, but to sing duets in between the contestants' singing. That was a fantastic break for me, and I duetted with Beverley Knight, Natasha Hamilton and Tony Christie. So even though Gregg and I were first out, a lot of good came out of the show. One day Stewart Copeland and I found ourselves walking along the studio corridor. I thought I would try to chat and warm him up a bit. Firstly I said how sorry I was to hear that his brother Ian, who had been my agent in the States, had died the year before of skin cancer.

When I met Ian in 1987, he was the most charming, funny and sexy guy. He'd fought in Vietnam and been awarded commendations and medals, and boy did he hope to get in your pants by telling you that. Then I told Stewart that I knew he'd been doing movie scores and compositions down the years. I said: 'I know you've really branched out since The Police but it would be great to see you drumming again. I loved The Police and your style reminds me of Keith Moon, it's flamboyant with lots of syncopation.' He thanked me for the compliment. Then he said: 'I've got this little band, a side project, we've got a few shows coming up.' And I said: 'Great, that's amazing, let me know when you're playing I'd love to come and see you.' He said: 'Oh you'll hear about it.' Still I did not twig. I couldn't help but notice, as we parted company, that he did not ask me one question about myself or what I was doing. He really didn't give a shit. According to him, as he said frequently throughout the series, only Beverley Knight could really sing on the show. When Bev and I duetted on Satisfaction by The Stones, we both took the roof off the place, but if you'd listened to Stewart you'd have thought that only Bev was singing. Beverley Knight is a superlative singer but I am no slouch myself, and he really offended me. Beverley had told me how much she liked my voice, we sang well together, but he seemed at pains to constantly belittle my voice.

And of course the 'little side project band' was the fucking Police reunion tour. And I just thought: 'You smarmy twat.' He'd said it with no humour, no wink, no twinkle in his eye. He played me for a sucker and was showing off by saying: 'I'm in this little band.' He made me feel so stupid.

Aside from the duets, the other high point of JTTOU was making a new and lasting friendship with TV presenter and actress Janet Ellis. Just as when Jennie and I sat beside each other on induction day at art school and never stopped talking and giggling, Janet and I were exactly the same when we met on the show. Janet was partnered up with Alexander O'Neal. Alexander has had well-documented substance abuse issues and they'd clearly taken a toll.

I have to confess that I have been lured to meetings by my Svengali-like agent David Samuel to be seen for both Celerity Big Brother and I'm

A Celebrity (or Minor Celebrity as it's called in our house) Get Me Out Of Here. I always say: 'No Way! ' But he swings a fob watch in front of my eyes and hypnotises me: 'It's just a meeting Carol, take the meeting, never hurts to just to take a meeting, so and so got tons of gigs after doing it and a 50k fee, just take the meeting.' But I never got the gigs, and I've never been so insulted as to be overlooked for rubbish TV. When I see the hideous self-obsessed wannabes and poor old Z-listers on the show, I always think 'what? I'm not good enough for this crap? Or am I not horrible enough? Am I too far below Z-list now?'

But on both those occasions my not being 'quite right' was a Godsend, because I may have done it! Everyone has their price and mine is remarkably low. I'd have been a total hypocrite as every year I sit there, drinking wine, perversely addicted to that car crash TV and slagging everyone off from the comfort of my sofa.

In 2007 my friend, promoter David Hartfield started up 'Rewind Festival – The '80s Festival.'

I had first worked with David in The Princess Diana Memorial Concert at Althrop, her family home. It was a privilege to sing China with The BBC Concert Orchestra. Scarlett was just three weeks old and strapped to my chest in a papoose carrier until I stepped on stage. I'd had what's called an 'elective induction.' The little monkey wouldn't come out and was a week overdue, and I was not missing that show. Even when we induced her, she still would not come out. As I mentioned before, I had a 24-hour labour, she got stuck in the birth canal and came out with a cone head. She also put paid to my trampolining career or the ability to laugh or cough without peeing myself for about four years. Now that I've mentioned that, I'm sure I'll get gifted a box of Tena Lady.

Anyway, many years later I reconnected with David as he also lives in Henley. I suggested to David that he should get in on the '80s thing. Rewind was born in 2007 and has not looked back. The brand travels all over world and now has three massive festivals in the UK. It has become not just a niche '80s monster, but a bona fide festival by anyone's standards, with Henley now having a 40,000 strong audience. I have now performed at nine Rewind Festivals, and it's a welcome opportunity for me to get back on a Shock and Awe stage. It's always a treat to see thousands and thousands of arms doing the '80s ballad wave as I perform China, and to feel the power of so many people singing along to my songs.

Rewind also compensated for the end of my acting career, which sadly fell by the wayside. I got fed up being the nearly girl and having moved 45 miles out of London, it was a drag to schlepp back in for auditions. When I'd co-starred in Mum's The Word, I'd had a 15-minute Tube ride into theatre land. For a while, I'd been determined to step up. To improve my chances of success, I'd gone to see another agent and she'd made it clear that if she was to take me on, I needed to take weekly drama classes in addition to singing lessons each alternate week, so that I could perfect a musical-style singing voice. But it wasn't for me. I hate that generic, brittle musical theatre sound. I like personality in a voice, and not just range. I have had offers over the years to tour musicals, but I could not make that long-term commitment to leaving my kids for months on end. I have to be able to manipulate my schedule around my family, they come first. Well, wine comes first, but then they definitely come next.

Back In 2011, I got a call from my friend Lucy who works in TV. She'd had the heads up that China was to be performed on ITV's X Factor, by a young contestant called Amelia Lily who was only 17. We don't watch the X Factor very often in our house, we're all a bit over it, but I thought it would be a great showcase for the song and hopefully for me. I told the kids that the song would feature, and we all agreed to sit down and watch the show. We were ready with the wine and the beer, the chips and the dips, and the apple juice and pretzels. Amelia came on and she gave a good performance. She was only 17 and China is a hard song to sing. I should know, I was 28 when I recorded it. I think you need an element of maturity in your voice to do it well. Amelia was good, but not great, and I won't lie, I have to admit that I was slightly relieved. Although it was a creditable performance, she wasn't better than me. China is my baby, after all. As the song faded, the cameras moved across to the judging panel. Gary Barlow was on the panel and he complimented

Amelia Lily on her performance. He said he remembered the original and 'it was nice to hear it sung in tune if I'm honest'.

For a split second I actually couldn't breathe. The children looked at me and began to get upset for me. Richard was astonished. We could not believe what we were witnessing. Where in the holy fuck did that come from? Gary's job was to critique her performance not have a go at me. It was hurtful, unnecessary and untrue! I'd had a couple of glasses of wine and I hit Twitter. I said: 'What the fuck is your problem Barlow?'

I don't know Gary, neither have I ever had a problem with him. I have been at the same events as Take That and chatted to some of the others but not met him. After my Twitter rant, my mobile phone rang off the hook in seconds. First it was the Xtra Factor asking: 'Will you come on the show and talk to Gary on the phone?' I said: 'Absolutely, bring it on.' Then several tabloid newspapers called: 'What do you think about your song getting on the biggest entertainment show in the UK and then you being slagged off by Gary at the end of it?'

I was angry and upset. I'd also had a couple of drinks so I was on the warpath. The Xtra Factor appearance didn't pan out: I was told that Gary wouldn't come to the phone. The next day on Radio 1, Edith Bowman said he was hiding in his dressing room and didn't want to come out. That day, I got a lame tweet from Gary saying: 'So sorry Carol, unnecessary and uncalled for.' But I think he should have apologised properly and we should have done a duet together. A few weeks later, I did a show called Christian O'Connell's Beer And Cake Club, at the Leicester Square Theatre. It was with Absolute Radio's Christian O'Connell and actor David Tennant. I sang Want You Back For Good, beautifully in tune, I might add. I finished by saying: 'Take That, Barlow.' Everybody pissed themselves laughing.

Pleasure And Pain

We got the old T'Pau line-up back together after a conversation between Ronnie and I. In 2012, I spoke to Ronnie and I said: 'Look, everybody's touring their seminal album. We ought to do that. What do you think?' Ronnie had done a few gigs through the years with me, like the 2011 Rewind Christmas tour. We'd also done a little digital single release, called Just Dream, in 2007. He'd also got his own thing going with his studio in Wales and his band The Ronaldos. He spent a lot of time producing and engineering, as well as developing young artists, a time-intensive task which could take a year from his life. I told him that if I was going to do a 25th anniversary tour of BOS, he absolutely had to do it too. He was the other founding member of T'Pau. We put the band together and were the principal songwriters. It would have been great if the original line-up could have got back together, but that wasn't going to happen. Besides, I had a great line-up in the band with Anthony Clarke on keys, Kez Günesh on bass, James Ashby on lead guitar, Ronnie on rhythm guitar and Dave Hattee, my drummer of eight years. So we got back together, booking 30 shows around the UK and totally rocking it. I finally succumbed to getting an au pair so that Dylan and Scarlett were in safe hands. I have to admit, I was terrified leaving my kids alone. The first au pair, Anita, was Hungarian and she was so dull that the kids were a bit miserable. I didn't like her at all, but she fulfilled her duties and was OCD about the cleaning, so the house was immaculate. But there was no interaction with the kids, other than getting them up for school and fed. Richard, my husband, also came on the road with us, tour managing the show. So it made me feel really bad that the kids were a bit unhappy, though at least they were safe. Midway through the tour, we'd booked a week's break. Anita took the opportunity to go shopping but after an hour I got a text to say she was ill and was going back to Hungary – NOW. I called: there was no reply. I texted: there was no reply. Suddenly it dawned on me to check her room, and all the wardrobes and drawers were empty. She had clearly planned it. I flew into a panic as I had five days to get someone else in before we got back on the road. We had been advised to get an older girl in to help. But Anita had been 30. She had spoken perfect English and had worked in the UK in care homes and as a security guard. We thought we'd already got somebody who had been up to the task. The only girl the agency could find to replace her was a 19-year-old French student, called Corally. Richard picked her up from Paddington. Corally was 6ft tall and from New Caledonia, a French island near Australia. Her English was pretty good, but a bit patchy. She couldn't cook so the kids ate a lot of toast. Housework did not really register with her, either, so the house quickly became a tip. Her room was messier than the kids'. But she was the loveliest girl and had personality in spades, so had buckets of energy and endless time for the children. We miss her to this day. So much for hiring a grown-up.

We hit the road for the second leg of the tour, confident in the knowledge that the children were happy.

The gigs went really well. We made money, everyone got paid and we were selling t-shirts and albums rapidly. I was in demand for countless TV and radio shows to promote it. Everything was great. And that's when the fans asked Ronnie and I to please record some new songs. Ron and I never like to say we're back together permanently, because we don't know where our futures might lead. Professionally speaking, we're both cool being together and apart. But there was so much demand that we thought: 'Let's get in the studio and do it.' So in the spring of 2014, we gathered the band together to work out a budget and start recording our new album Pleasure And Pain.

We recorded at Ronnie's studio, in Monmouth. It was the first T'Pau record since Red and with 15 years between albums, my output had not been that consistent. There had been many reasons for that. I hadn't put a record out in years because that would have meant promoting it, schlepping around the clubs, and paying promotional teams to get it playlisted on radio – it was an almost impossible task. I no longer had a big label to advance the funds for all of that, so anything new was down

to me, financially-speaking. Plus I just didn't have the enthusiasm or
energy and nobody seemed interested in me making a record anyway. I'd
lost confidence in that side of my career. I was earning good money on
the '80s festival circuit, so I didn't feel compelled to put myself under
that pressure. All people seemed to want to hear was the old hits, so I
just relaxed and went with that. I didn't feel particularly creative, either,
and I also found that having two small children to look after meant I had
enough commitments. I couldn't do all my shows then disappear into the
studio to start making new music. It's very intense being in the studio and
I didn't want to hand my kids over to nannies.

Ronnie and I had written a lot of songs down the years. When we
parted company, for instance, we had dozens of half-finished songs that
were left to gather dust. We'd done many demoing sessions when we
owned Newgrove Farm, in Monmouth, too. So we harvested the best bits
from some of the best songs that we'd written in the early 1990s. We gave
them new choruses and brought them back to life. A lot of them had a
really good verse, a really good b-verse and then fell down a hole when
it came to the important bit, the please-don't-bore-us-give-us-the-chorus.
Ronnie and I now felt inspired. Some songs came really quickly, and
some songs were like pulling teeth. We sat for six hours one day getting
one line right on a song. Remarkably, it was worth all the hair-pulling as
it ended up as House Of Love, a fabulous track. Other songs just came
flying out of our pens and I had already written Read My Mind. That was
always destined for the album.

One night in the studio, the day long done, we were jamming after a
few beers. Nowhere, a beautiful power ballad, was born. The beauty of
digital recording is that if you get it right, it goes down almost straight
away. Sometimes that first shot is the take that makes the record. You
capture the spontaneity. It feels very real, and very alive. My Mum was
delighted that we were recording. For years, she would nag me to death
about getting back in the studio. She knew I'd lost my confidence, and she
thought the best way to get it back was to record again.

Every time I went up to visit, she'd have all my old demo tapes and
would play them, preferring the rockier tunes. She liked the original

version of Demolition Man, but we didn't think the chorus was strong enough so we wrote a great new chorus for it.

Sadly Mum became really ill when I was in the studio recording Pleasure And Pain.

We had a tour booked in to promote it, starting in October 2014, and we were all set to finish the album and get on the road. In September, Mum got an infection called cellulitis, which is a deep tissue infection and that turned into sepsis, or, blood poisoning. Over the last 10 years, Mum had become more and more unwell. She'd had heart failure and kidney failure. She was on at least a dozen tablets a day. The pills to help with her heart impacted badly on her kidneys and vice versa. It was hard to get the balance right, the side effects of the drugs seemed worse than the ailments they were meant to treat. She was frequently in hospital, under yet another consultant, who would try to fine-tune her meds. She felt nauseous all the time, every single day. It was very hard to get consistent treatment, as we saw several different consultants and had to start at the beginning again and again, reviewing her past care before we could move forward. Different consultants had different ideas on what should be done. Sometimes her care was pedestrian and demotivating, and sometimes a bright new young doctor would be working at the hospital and have a fresh and energetic approach on her complicated medical condition. He would re-jig everything and Mum would feel much better for another six months.

Our family grew accustomed to Mum never being very well, and we joked she was like a creaking gate; she never got fixed but was never actually broken. Mum was very stubborn and just refused to give in, but she was very fragile at the same time. Over the last five years of her life, the constant roller coaster of ill health and hospitalisation took its toll on us, her children. My brother and his wife lived close by, so a lot of responsibility fell on their shoulders. It caused tension that I was so far away and could do less to help. I felt very guilty that I couldn't be there more often, and I resented them not understanding the strain that put on me. I also thought, sometimes, that if I was the one who lived closer, there were some things that I would have done that they didn't and so it went.

I would live in fear of the phone ringing, as with each passing month it became clear that we would not be receiving any good news. I had the added strain of being two hours away. On a daily basis I simply could not do as much as they did.

It was tough to balance everything, and there were occasions when I had to tell my brother that I couldn't be there sometimes because of gigs and other commitments. I too had work, children at school who had to be supervised, a home to run, a hard-working husband. I couldn't always just drop everything, and as he lived closer he just had to be practical about it. If it was a real emergency, then of course I dropped everything.

However, the reality was that we all did a lot for my Mum. We are an argumentative bunch in my family, and sometimes it's as exhausting as an episode of Jeremy Kyle. We remain critical of each other's actions at times, but we did actually all rally round in our different ways. They call us the sandwich generation: we have ailing, elderly relatives, and dependant children. We're caught in the middle. It's hard for everyone. Plus my brother and I have always had a feisty relationship. We both have very strong personalities and won't back down in a fight.

Mum also became very difficult to be around. She was very aggressive and grumpy, and it wasn't just the strain of feeling unwell. She was different. Her mind didn't work the same way as it once did. She would argue and then contradict herself in a split second. I did not know what she was talking about half the time. I didn't realise until she was actually dying. When we spoke to her two new consultants, they provided a reason for it, explaining that she had vascular dementia. I felt truly awful, as there had been times when I had been very short with her, particularly when she'd been difficult to be around. My mind returned to the occasions when we had driven to see her and Scarlett would tell me: 'Please don't shout at Nanny today.' That makes me feel dreadful and I have to live with that now. I am not a patient person. I loved her very much, but she drove me nuts sometimes and when I realised she couldn't help it, it was too late.

The staff at The George Elliot Hospital in Nuneaton were, in the main, fantastic, though like every large hospital in the NHS system there were some failings and mistakes. Mum was twice on a ward closed down by the Norovirus, and she was once discharged with it and gave it to me.

Mum was treated for her cellulitis in A&E and was then discharged. She collapsed the next day, and the paramedics who arrived in the ambulance were aghast that she had been discharged as she clearly had severe sepsis. So I couldn't help wondering if a more vigilant doctor or nurse in that A&E department might have spotted that, and admitted her then. Who knows what the outcome might have been if they had? Maybe she would have survived. Your mind goes everywhere in times like those, and you instinctively wonder whether everyone has done the best they could.

Mum went into intensive care towards the end of September 2014, and I spent the next three weeks dashing to be with her and my brother, racing back via Monmouth to finish the album, and trying to get home to see my kids. Ronnie was nose-to-the-grindstone on his own, working on the post-production, though he obviously needed my input. I would stay at my Mum's house, which was comforting as I could feel her in every room. But it was also sad, as part of me suspected that she wasn't going to go home again. I would smell her clothes hanging up in the wardrobe and sleep in her big cardie. Scarlett and I wear them at home now. They live on the sofa for our popcorn and TV nights, and I still haven't washed them a year later. I knew in my heart that my mother had made her awful last journey to hospital and would never return to her much-loved house again. She had been very happy there.

In the last week of September, I called my agent and told him to pull the Pleasure And Pain tour because I could not cope. I couldn't get the album finished in time for the tour and I was starting to unravel. On October the 1st, I had come home from Nuneaton via Monmouth after a day in the studio. I desperately needed to see my kids and feel normal for a day. The phone rang at home about 11.30am, and it was Claire, my sister-in-law. She said Mum had gone downhill rapidly and I had better get back there right away. I got dressed quickly, jumped straight in the car and drove without recalling the journey at all. I was transported back to the day my father died in 1990, when I had dashed from Monmouth to

The George Elliot, not recalling a moment of how I got there.

They had flushed Mum's kidneys through twice on filter and she had rallied for a few days. All of her relatives came from far and wide. She was galvanised by all the attention and company. She was laughing and really chatty, and we were hopeful. But part of me worried that she was so infirm, she had nowhere left to rally to. My brother had been to see a few care homes but had been depressed by what he found.

Mum could no longer sit up. She had to be lifted out of bed by a painful pulley system. She couldn't go to the loo and had reverted back to being a toddler in nappies. Her diet was yoghurt. It was so undignified and it broke my heart. I wanted her to let go, for her – and for us.

During these few lucid days, I got to play her some rough mixes from the album. She had sufficient presence of mind to be really pleased. She was thrilled that finally, after all those years, I was back in the studio with Ronnie. I popped my headphones on her head and she sang very loudly and out of tune along to Nowhere, Sammy and Dave, and Demolition Man, a track she had always loved.

Her recovery was short-lived. I arrived at the hospital at almost 2pm on October 2nd 2014 and Mum was on life-support. A machine was assisting her breathing, literally pushing air into her lungs. Her eyes were closed, and she was making the strangest constant repetitive noise. She was locked inside herself. It was made clear to my brother and I that this was the end. The machine was keeping her alive by inflating her lungs. We could sit with her for as long as we liked, and the doctors told us it would be our call to switch it off. The nurses on intensive care wards are wonderfully compassionate people. They have to see families go through harrowing times and it must take its toll on them. They also hate to lose a patient and they were fond of my Mum. She had been joking with them and barking at them for almost a month, and several of them knew her and my brother as though they were locals. Claire, Gary and I sat with her, and my brother and I each held her hand. The nurse told us to keep talking to her as apparently hearing is the last sense to go. We told her how much we loved her and what a fantastic mother and grandmother she had been. At 3pm, we told them to stop the machine and the nurse made her comfortable with a large dose of morphine. She stopped making the strange noise and her body relaxed. At 3.20pm our mother died. My daughter Scarlett was born at exactly 3.20pm. It was a coincidence, we could have called it at any time, but Scarlett loved the synchronicity. Not to put too fine a point on it, a body continues to let out air and the muscles twitch as everything subsides and switches off. Mum still appeared active. We looked at the nurse who gave us a sweet, understanding smile and said: 'She's gone.' My brother couldn't watch and had to leave the room. I stayed with her until she was still.

We cremated Mum on October 15th. She had been a rock'n'roll chick at heart. Being long-ago Catholics, we had an open casket at the funeral parlour and we called this her Meet and Greet. The service was referred to as The Gig and her wake was the After Show Party. Mum would have loved the informality and humour. It was so moving to see my brother, cousins, my husband, and Ronnie carry her coffin. We played Evergreen by Barbra Streisand as she had frequently stood to sing that at the piano, with our Dad accompanying her. My brother had composed a heart-felt and emotional poem to her. Unfortunately, it had the pentameter of a limerick and unbelievably, I felt myself again getting the inappropriate giggles.

We had an informal buffet and open bar at a local pub. We had stuck pictures of Mum that had been taken down the years all over the wall. They made for wonderful conversations as family and friends stood together and reminisced. There were a lot of tears and a lot of laughter. She was a big character and left a big gap. It's difficult to believe but a year has gone by as I write this. It's October 11th, 2015 and it's already a bit chilly, so I am wearing her big grey cardigan.

It's been very hard to let go of those final moments with her. I was so privileged – and glad for her – that I was able be with her as she left us, but still find it hard to lose that final haunting image of her dying face so that I can remember her in better times. I miss her every day and yes, I have to live with some guilt about certain things. You always think you'll have time to put a few things right.

I Got To Sing My Song

All in all, 2014 was a pretty bad year. Not long before my Mum died, I'd also fractured my ankle – though I didn't realise that for months. Let me explain how The Queen is part of this sorry tale.

On July 17th 2014, I had to be at Ritz Rehearsal Studios in Putney, London, to rehearse for the Rewind Festival. My plan was to jump on the train from Reading to Paddington, which takes 25 minutes, and then catch a 20-minute District Line connection to Putney Tube station. Ritz is two streets from there: easy, peasy, lemon-squeezy. I was due in Putney at 2pm.

What could possibly go wrong? Well, everything, or so it seemed. When I got to Reading Station, the entire new entrance was cordoned off with dozens of police and security hanging about, as well as some very cheap bunting and balloons. The Queen was there to open the new part of that very impressive station. Travellers were ushered around to the old side of the station where, of course, the queues to purchase tickets were as deep as an ocean. By the time I got a ticket, I was running 30 minutes late and I had to get on a 12.30pm train instead of the noon train. Finally I got to Paddington at 1 pm. I went down to the Tube and a flashing sign said: 'Closures on the Circle and District line, reduced service'. Fuck!

Finally a Tube train come along. I checked my watch: 1.15 pm. I called our MD, Richard Brook, and explained what had happened. He said they'd start to run the songs without me, but couldn't promise I'd have any extra time as the next artist would be arriving for their slot after me, and they had about 10 artists to rehearse that day. Everyone else was on schedule. I got to Putney Bridge at 1.35pm and started to jog from the station to the studio. Just as I reached the entrance my right ankle gave way and I fell sharply to my right. I quickly corrected myself to the left, and felt a sharp crack down the outside of my right ankle. I lay on the floor for about five minutes in agony. I'll never forget, a guy wearing headphones walked past and just looked at me rolling around before walking on. Finally I gathered myself together and limped into the studio crying. The band came to my assistance and the studio manager got me a big bag of ice. I elevated my foot up on a stool and took some of my emergency ibuprofen, which were stashed in my bag. The ice made my ankle numb, so I quickly did the rehearsal sitting down with my leg up. The studio drove me back to Putney Bridge and I visited a chemist nearby, where I bought a compression bandage. I strapped my ankle tightly, and using escalators and lifts, I somehow got back to Reading from where I drove home. My ankle very quickly became shockingly swollen, turning black and blue. But I soldiered on and thought it was just a very bad sprain that I would be able to sort out myself with 'RICE' treatment: Rest, Ice, Compress, Elevate. Besides, I did not have the time to sit for hours in the local A&E. It took a long time to heal, but gradually my ankle seemed to get slowly better. I had to strap it every day and could only limp around in trainers. June 18th was Richard's 50th birthday, and we had booked a four-day trip to Paris. We got The Metro and cabs to get about the city, but there was also some walking to do around the arrondissements, tourist attractions and beautiful parks. Paris is so architecturally stunning that the only way to really enjoy it is by being out there on the street. So living on a diet of painkillers, washed down with excellent French wine, we marched around gay Paris! Across the summer, I had to do various festivals, including Rewind with my ankle strapped, but I couldn't dance or move about much. So cut to December 2014, and we were on holiday in Europe skiing. My ankle was still tugging a bit and I still could only tolerate wearing trainers. It had also started to ache across the front now as well, getting worse rather than better. Ironically, I was actually okay skiing as the ski boot held my ankle in a neutral position, isolating any movement. But staggering around the bars at night really hurt.

Our postponed tour had been put back to the end of January 2015, and

Pleasure And Pain finally came out at the beginning of February. It gained excellent reviews on Amazon and iTunes. We hired a great PR in Lisa Davies Promo, and got some good radio play on Radio 2 with Graham Norton, Terry Wogan, Ken Bruce and my good buddy Kim Wilde on her Magic FM show. They all gave the lead-off single, Nowhere, a few national spins for us. We had wonderful support from long-standing fans, too. Tracy Gilchrist, AKA Stella-Bella, designed the album cover. Dean Hollet ran an official FB page for us and of course Ryan Ward out in the US of A, was running the website www.tpau.co.uk.

In rehearsal, two things were happening that caused me concern. Firstly, my throat felt constricted, and secondly, my ankle was still really painful, even though it was six months since I'd fallen. I went to see a medic who used ultrasound to look into the joint and she didn't like what she saw. So I booked a private MRI scan which revealed that I had two hairline fractures down the right-hand side. However, because it had gone untreated, I'd also now got a stress fracture across the front and had developed bone marrow edema. My bone was filling up with fluid, compressing the marrow, and the blood supply to my ankle was impaired. I had to get off my feet straight away, wear an air-walker boot – which was a bit like a lightweight ski boot – and use crutches. It was not good news for our rescheduled tour, but we tried to work around it by buying a nice Val Doonican stool for me to use on stage. I also found the sexiest flat boots that I could, which wasn't easy. I can't tell you how sad I was to be on stage without my standard issue killer heels. That was the most tragic part!

My consultant was not happy with my plans, however. She wanted me on strict bed or sofa rest, and explained that I could lose my ankle function if I didn't take her seriously. Her exact words were: 'I don't want to frighten you.' And then she proceeded to frighten me. I told her I had no choice but to play; I could not cancel the tour again. We negotiated that I would use my crutches and boot at all times; I would not lift a finger and the crew would practically carry me around. When I was on stage, I agreed to sit on my stool whenever possible.

There were other things troubling me. I felt pretty run down, I kept running a temperature and I was generally off my game and struggling to hit my notes. I tried not to sing too much in rehearsal, and hoped for the best when we hit the road. Both Richard and I had had flu jabs, but it was all over the news that the injections had only helped about three per cent of the population. Within a week of the tour starting, I'd developed full-blown flu, as had Richard. My throat became tight and swollen, and I just couldn't sing. We postponed some dates and I took to my bed for eight days. Things got worse, and I was diagnosed as having acute bronchitis. Having never previously heard the word edema, I was now to hear it twice. I went to see a top throat specialist in London. He stuck a camera up my nose and threaded it through to my throat, the most vile and uncomfortable procedure. I had to attempt a series of notes for him as he looked on the screen, but I could barely swallow let alone sing 'Ah.' He confirmed that I had vocal chord edema, which means my vocal chords were practically swollen shut. I was stunned, though he told me the good news was, that despite my having no voice at all, he could see no long-term damage. However, like the ankle specialist, he warned that if I didn't stop there and then, I ran the risk of long-term trouble. I had tried so hard to keep going, but I'd been run off the road. Most of our shows ran from Thursday to Sunday, so we hoped I could rest from Monday to Wednesday to recover. We'd tried that for a couple of weeks, but I didn't get enough sustained downtime to recover. Rather than feeling better, I was feeling worse by the day. I came out of his rooms and called my agent, Lee Noble, straight away. I gave him the prognosis and we put out a formal announcement that the tour was cancelled. I was gutted.

The promoters were going to be pissed off with a second postponement or possible cancellations. The band, though sympathetic, were naturally very disappointed. They had all prioritised T'Pau and turned down other work. Our fans however were amazing. I have cancelled only a handful of shows in almost 30 years, so they know they can rely on me to have a very good reason to cancel. I had numerous Tweets and Facebook messages of support. One or two promoters got a bit shitty and tried to get money from me, but I was genuinely covered by my consultant and doctor's notes.

On October 10th 2015, we finished a run of rescheduled shows from the Pleasure And Pain tour, and they utterly rocked as so many faithful fans had kept their tickets from two postponements. It meant so much to them – and us – to get those shows done. It had taken me six months to get my voice back fully but I was thrilled that I had.

Looking forward – I think the perspective I now have is that I know my story isn't any different to anybody else's. I have had my ups and downs, my great moments and my sorrows.

For years I wallowed in self-pity, and I failed to realise that I've had a lot of good luck in my life. I've had real good fortune because there are lots of people out there who don't get the breaks. Most backing singers I know can sing me under the table, but it's about having a bit of spark; that's what makes people take an interest in you.

For too long, I defined myself by what I perceived as my failure because the original T'Pau crashed and burned, and I've never had a hit record since.

It's been very difficult to define myself by that success, and instead I reverted to defining myself by what went wrong. Will Ashurst, my friend and former manager, once said to me: 'Why is the cup always half empty, Carol? Why can't you enjoy what you've achieved in a very tricky business and pat yourself on the back?'

It's a defence mechanism, I guess. I will put myself down before others have the opportunity to. I was an insecure, nervous child at school, and that person is still in there somewhere. The nasty bitches at school burned me, when they ostracised me. The cruel maths teacher who told me I didn't deserve my place at a grammar school made me feel worthless and inadequate; and the smart–arsed and cowardly music journalists and sour critics defeated my creative spirit. I had no real self-confidence, only bravado. I remember, many years back, I was in a black cab going to an interview with Mariella Frostrup, and I was whining about someone slagging me off. She became quite impatient with me, then gave it to me straight. She told me that she'd encountered the same problem but because she was smart, pretty and ambitious, she'd got over it. She told me I was in the same boat, that I should stop whingeing and just get over it because it came with the territory. I never had her brass balls then, but I know now she was right. Not everyone is going to like you, you have to grow up and get over it.

When I was very successful and famous, it superficially fixed the problem for a while without really solving it. When my great success with T'Pau was over, the public rejected me professionally, and then Ronnie rejected me personally. It was a double whammy. I've had many bouts of depression. Depression renders you impotent and you can't function. You can't see the wood for the trees, and you have no appreciation of the positives in your life. Depression makes you self-absorbed and self-centred.

I've taken the pills; I've had therapy and counselling; I have had bouts of self-medicating with booze. What's the saying? 'Poor me, poor me, pour me another drink'.

Most people have been bullied at some point in their life, ignored or rejected. We've all been through these things, but as my Mum used to say, I was such a drama queen. My dramas always felt so intense that they consumed me. I turned a lot of them into songs.

So coming full circle: in my family, I have my safe harbour. I went from being allergic to children to being the most hands-on, over-protective lioness of a mother that a kid can have. Scarlett and Dylan have to tell me to back off, because if anyone upsets them I want to go and beat them up. I have developed such courage on their behalf that I never had for myself as child. They have brought a whole new dimension to my life and I love them so. Dylan is a card and he's like me. If you open the fridge door, he does 20 minutes. He's really funny and a show-off. Scarlett is artistic, thoughtful but cautious. They are both a bit crazy, but then they are my kids.

And as for my husband Richard: when I met him, the first thing that struck me – apart from the fact that I fancied him like mad – was that he had such a sense of himself. He had such deep-rooted self-confidence. He's not afraid of anything. He always says there's a solution to everything.

He is my best mate, my lover and my confidant. I was even able to talk to him about Ronnie, and he was so secure in himself and so confident of my love for him, that he was able to absorb that and understand my need to divest that pain.

I needed to articulate my feelings so that Richard could know who I was. He's never felt threatened at all by the enormous history and connection that Ronnie and I still have.

He said to me one day, when I talked about doing this book and was unsure how much I should write about the personal side, to just go for it. He simply smiled and said: 'I am aware you shared a bed.' And he genuinely likes Ronnie, and Ronnie genuinely likes him. I have my two favourite men in my life.

So right now all is good. I have my off days like anyone else, but I only have to look around me and pull myself into check.

I now like doing different things. I'm mixing it up. I remember how Kylie once said she only had to follow her hot pants around.

I got the gag; I think I follow China In Your Hand around. It's kind of flipped. It's not me that pulls the crowd anymore, the song has taken on a life of its own. One week I'm playing in a riotous gay bar, a theatre or a grungy rock club band, then I'm playing The Isle Of Wight Festival for 20,000 people.

I've got more TV coming up. I have had my name up in lights on the West End stage, I've hosted radio shows, written newspaper articles . . . and . . . oh, I'm writing an autobiography right now!

I have never been so busy. I've learned to duck and dive and enjoy the ebb and flow.

I get enjoyment out of everything, instead of constantly comparing it to the old days. I have only recently stopped seeing myself as a failed pop star, and can now acknowledge myself as a creative writer and singer of songs, and a seasoned performer.

I dug myself so deeply into that pit of fame in order to feel that I existed, that I couldn't dig myself out without help. I was lucky that my family and good friends were there for me; they love me for being the beautiful-but-flawed asshole that I am.

I've accepted that I had a glorious moment in the sun. I am grateful I had it at all, and I am not embarrassed that I did not sustain it.

The 18th century American philosopher and poet, Henry Thoreau, said: 'Most men live lives of quiet desperation, and go to the grave with the song still in them.' I got to sing my song.